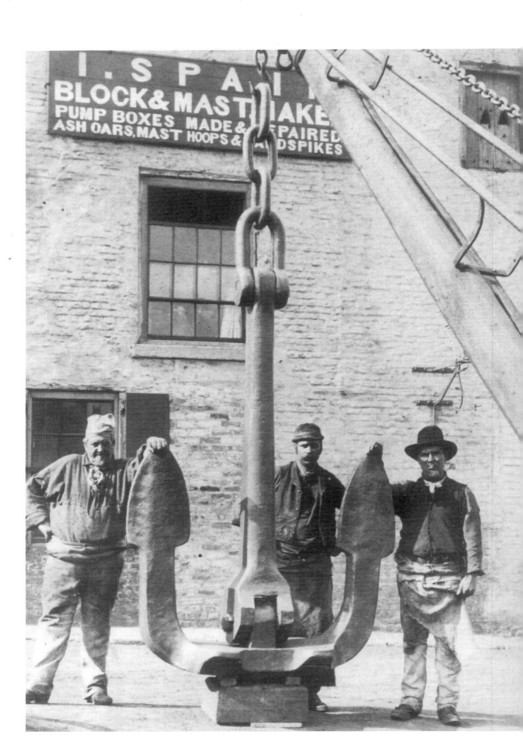

1899

ANCHORS

AN ILLUSTRATED HISTORY

Betty Nelson Curryer

CHATHAM PUBLISHING

LONDON

Dedicated to

Captain Neville E Upham,
Younger Brother of Trinity House,
Master in the Union Castle Mail Steamship Line,
Member of the Association of Old Worcesters
with the author's warmest thanks for his generosity in making
available all his research material on the subject.

Frontispiece
Anchormen: workers from W L Byers' Sunderland foundry
pose with the company's Patent 'Reliance' Stockless
Anchor, about 1890. *(Tyne & Wear Museums)*

Copyright © Betty Nelson Curryer 1999

First published in Great Britain in 1999
by Chatham Publishing,
61 Frith Street, London W1V 5TA

Chatham Publishing is an imprint of
Gerald Duckworth & Co Ltd

British Library Cataloguing in Publication Data
A catalogue record for this book is available from the
British Library

ISBN 1 86176 080 9

Typeset and design by Tony Hart

Printed and bound in Great Britain by
WBC Book Manufacturers Ltd

Contents

Acknowledgements

With thanks to friends and colleagues in the
National Maritime Museum at Greenwich for
patiently answering questions and indicating lines
of research. Most especially, thanks to Mrs Janet
Barber, Head of the Maritime Resources Group, for
moral support and unfailing kindness. A warm
'thank you' to Mr Brian Lavery, who having early
undergone the trauma of preparing a book, managed to listen sympathetically to the author's pleas
for reassurance. Thanks, too, to the staff of the
Caird Library, who unfailingly produced, sometimes after considerable trouble, the books the
author requested for reference.

It goes without saying that the author is particularly grateful for the use of prints in the collection of
the National Maritime Museum as illustarations to
the book.

Lastly, to Chatham Publishing, and Mr Rob
Gardiner in particular, my appreciation of the steer-
ing hand that guided me through unfamiliar waters.

Introduction:
Anchors and their use

The anchor is one of the earliest artifacts made by man – and for purely peaceful purposes. The stone anchor that secured his craft prior to and during the Bronze Age is still used today close to shore by fishermen around the world, and especially in the eastern Mediterranean. Developed through time into 'the large heavy iron instrument which dropped from a ship into the bottom of the sea keeps her in a proper situation from being driven away by the wind or tide' (William Falconer, *Universal Dictionary of the Marine*, 1769), the anchor is arguably the most important piece of safety equipment, without which no prudent mariner would take to the seas.

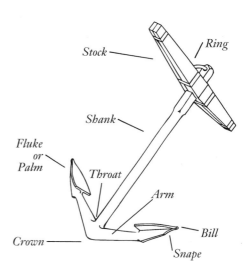

The parts of a standard 'Admiralty' pattern anchor. (Author)

Today the anchor is familiar to landsmen and seamen alike as an emblem on cap badges, public house signs and heraldic splendours; long considered a sign of hope in Christian civilisations, it is often chosen by individuals to mark their homes, and their final resting places. Colloquially, anyone retiring from the sea is said to have 'swallowed the anchor'. Notice that a fouled anchor is usually represented, *ie* one with the cable twined round the shank, thus prompting unfavourable comment from the sailors struggling to raise it. On personal coats of arms the fouling cable may be variously rendered – as a serpent presumably slain by the bearer, or as the Aldine printing house's elegant dolphin. Notice, too, that these emblems cannot show

Aldine anchor

The action of the modern
stockless anchor.
(Author)

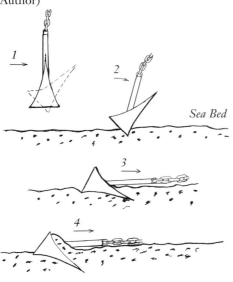

clearly that arms and stock are at right-angles to each other, so that the flukes (also known as palms) dig into the sea bed while the stock, lying roughly flat, increases the drag on the anchor. If both were in the same plane the whole would be free to slide ineffectively.

Chinese literature does offer an early mention of ships furnished with oars, rudders and anchors in use about 2000 BC, but tracing their growth from the simplest form must start with the stone anchors of Chapter 1. And it demands an almost impossible leap of the imagination from these to the huge steel anchors, some weighing 30 tons, carried by the VLCCs (very large crude carriers) of today, but this is where the latter began.

How the Anchor Holds

After defining the 'heavy iron instrument', as noted earlier, William Falconer entered a significant caveat: 'The action of an anchor can only be comprehended by experiment, and, by the kindness of Providence, seems to be governed by laws peculiar to itself and adapted to its use.' David Steel, author of *Elements & Practice of Rigging and Seamanship* written in 1794, was much more down to earth. 'Anchors are strong crooked instruments, made of iron and wood; used at sea, in rivers, roads etc. to retain ships and vessels from danger, or keep them in a convenient station,' he wrote firmly, as if defying them to do their worst.

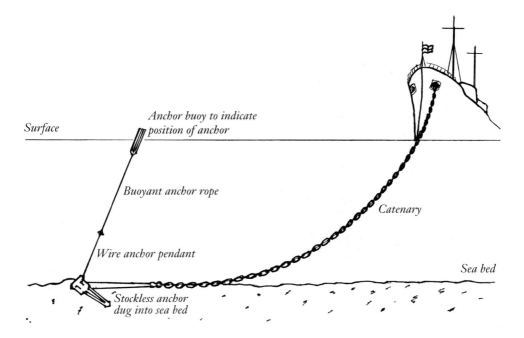

Surface

Anchor buoy to indicate position of anchor

Buoyant anchor rope

Catenary

Wire anchor pendant

Sea bed

Stockless anchor dug into sea bed

These 'heavy iron instruments' and their successors held to the sea bed not only because their flukes dug deeply into it, but because the proper length of cable attaching anchor to ship in itself augmented the holding power. Too short a cable which does not allow the long curve from ship's bows to anchor on the sea bed–the curve known as the catenary–weakens or defeats the anchor's purpose. It is generally accepted that roughly three to five times the depth of water in which the ship lies is a proper basis for calculating the cable's length. It is also considered that if the ship is in trouble from a sudden hard blow that one anchor with a long cable will give a surer hold than many with cables of insufficient length.

The catenary is essential for two reasons, the first being that the deeper the curve the more horizontal the eventual pull on the anchor, which tends to bury the anchor flukes deeper into the ground. The second is that with the elasticity provided by a deep curve in the cable a vessel is preventing from snubbing to her anchor as she rides to a sea (snubbing may be defined as bringing the vessel to a sudden stop, as when letting go an anchor with too much way on). For this reason chain cable is better than rope, quite apart from the likelihood of damage to

How the anchor holds. (Author)

An original drawing showing one of the first scientific attempts at calculating holding power of anchors, comparing Rodger's Long- and Short-Shank models with Pering's Improved, 1839. (National Maritime Museum DR7693)

the latter through chafing. A chain cable must be lifted gradually because of its weight, and so the ship is stopped easily without the shock of a surge. Using the maximum cable that local conditions permit has always been recommended: 'Old fishermen ride out a storm by putting out a light storm anchor far to windward with a very long cable.'

Writing this in *The Nautical Magazine* in May 1844, Mr W Walker RN, the Queen's Harbourmaster at Plymouth, went on to suggest that the effects of anchorage ground should be taken into consideration and better understood. 'If, for example, a large-palmed anchor start in Portland Roads, such is the stiffness of the soil that large lumps will adhere to the palm and prevent it taking hold a second time . . . hence the old practice of treating it with tallow.' He adds that the anchor's hold will be augmented the deeper it penetrates into clay or mud, as the fluke and arm leave a vacuum behind. So the weight of mud, of the column of water above it, and of the atmosphere on the sea surface augment the difficulty in weighing the anchor, even if the cable is up and down. At this point there is a name that will become familiar: 'As a machine for hooking on to the bottom of the sea, and retaining a ship in her position, Lt Rodger's anchor has not been surpassed. Its small palm would induce one to believe that such an anchor could not be a good one, but the fact is, that this palm is big enough for fishing the anchor, and just large enough and of such a form as to cause the arm to dive into the mud . . . where the adhesion of the soil must be enormous.'

This process of weighing, allowing for contemporary commands, can hardly have changed although modern equipment has taken it over. The novelist Alexander Fullerton describes it thus:

> The cable comes clanking in with regular metallic crashes as each iron link bangs out of the hawse hole, followed by the cry from the focsle 'Cable's up and down!' This signifies that all the slack of the cable has been dragged inboard, the cable is now vertical so that the next few turns of the capstan will break the anchor out of the sea bed. The command 'Weigh' follows and the clanking starts up again. Finally, the response 'Anchors aweigh!' followed by 'Clear anchor!' meaning that the anchor can now be seen, free of cable or wire fouling it.

Catting and Fishing

Compared with the process just described, stowing the older stocked anchor was difficult and dangerous – and more so in the case of the Porter and Trotman types with 'horns' on the outside of the arms. This was possibly a reason for the rejection of these anchors by the Navy Board; it certainly hastened the development of the stockless anchor and the hawse hole.

Once weighed the Old Longshank or Admiralty anchor had to be lifted clear of the water. A tackle fixed to the end of a stout beam jutting from the ship's bow was hooked on to the anchor ring or shackle. This tackle usually had a threefold purchase,

The process of catting (left) and fishing an anchor as carried out in the age of sail. The cable has been omitted for clarity. (From Darcy Lever's Young Sea Officer's Sheet Anchor, 1819)

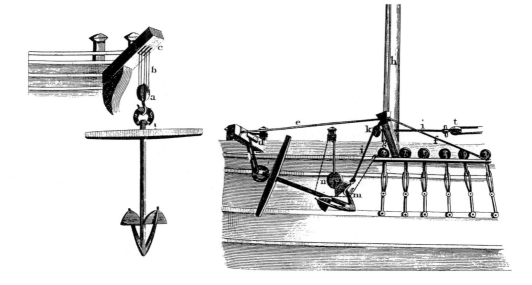

with the upper block formed by sheaves in the cathead, and the lower by the cat-block, with a strong hook under it. The name 'cathead' derived from the fashion of painting or carving a feline mask on the outer end of the beam. This was at first, around 1500, portable, and protruded through the 'cathole' in the chosen side of the ship. A century later it seems to have been a fixture, certainly in larger vessels.

Once hove up to the cathead and hanging vertically (*ie* catted), the anchor was then hoisted to the horizontal close to the ship's side. This was by means of a fish davit, hooked on at the crown of the anchor, or later, a fishbuckle on the anchor's shank. 'Billboards', or planked panels, were fixed to the ship's hull, so preventing damage by the anchor's flukes. So 'the anker was catted and fysshed', as recorded in the early fifteenth century. When the process was reversed to let go an anchor, it was first suspended vertically from the cathead; the anchor was then said to be 'A-Cockbill'.

The cat and fish tackle of a mid nineteenth-century wooden warship. (From George Nares' Seamanship, 1883 edition)

The fish davit is recorded as early as the fifteenth century: the *Christopher* of 1410-1412 had a davit on her focsle, as had the *Mary de la Toure*, along with two hooks, two hoops and two 'catte' hooks. Smaller craft of the Henry VII period (1485-1509) had only ropes and hooks to fish the anchor. One of the

Catting and fishing an Admiralty pattern anchor in an ironclad. (From George Nares' Seamanship, 1883 edition)

ship's boats at this period had a 'davyot' for weighing anchors by means of the buoy rope.

Note that in eighteenth-century vessels the fish tackle was run from a portable beam which could be transferred easily from one side of the ship to the other.

In the middle of the nineteenth century the introduction of

Anchor stowage on an inclined bed. (From McDermaid's Shipyard Practice, 1917)

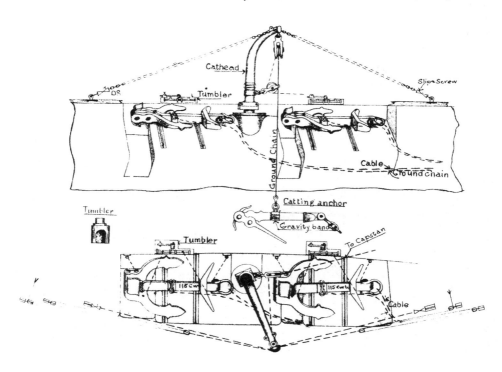

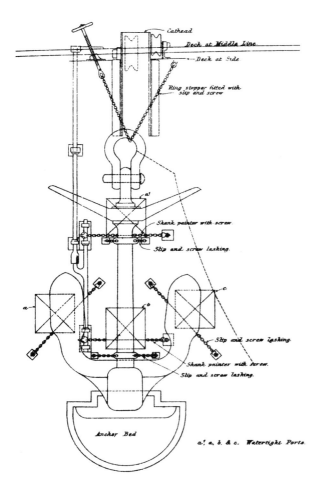

Cathead

Deck at Middle Line

Deck at Side

Ring stopper fitted with slip and screw

Shank painter with screw.

Slip and screw lashing.

Slip and screw lashing.

Shank painter with screw.

Slip and screw lashing.

Anchor Bed

a! a, b, & c. Watertight Ports.

Vertical stowage of a Martin's Improved Anchor. (From The Manual of Seamanship for Boys and Seamen of the Royal Navy, 1904)

larger iron and steel ships, in parallel with the newer 'close stowing' forms of anchor, necessarily led to revised methods of handling anchors. In ironclad warships the bowers were often stowed on a flat but inclined bed, but they still required an anchor davit for the equivalent of catting and fishing. Smaller ships, like cruisers, employed a form of vertical stowage on the side of the hull forward. The awkward nature of such systems gave impetus to the development of stockless anchors which could be drawn up simply into a hawse hole, the method which is still most commonly used in anything bigger than small craft.

Kedging

The practice of kedging, (that is, enabling a vessel to move in comparatively shallow water without the use of her own means of propulsion) seems to have been familiar for several centuries. Captain John Smith in his *Sea Grammar* of 1627 described the function of three types of anchor. The kedge or kedger, the smallest, was for working a ship up or down a river or inlet. In 1599 an Italian traveller, Aquillante Rochetta, witnessed a practical demonstration of kedging. Through lack of wind his ship was delayed in Alexandria, so her anchors were lowered into a dinghy and rowed out to the length of her cables. The vessel then used her own capstan to haul herself to the position of her anchors. This was repeated till the ship caught the wind and could move freely under her own sails. [*Voyages en Egypt des annees 1579-1601*, Editions Sauneron (IFAO Cairo 1974)]

Weighing Anchor in an Eighteenth-century Ship of the Line

The anchor cable of a 74-gun ship of the line was about 18 inches in circumference, and therefore too heavy and unmanageable to take around a capstan. To heave on the cable and thus weigh the anchor, a smaller endless rope, termed the messenger, went round the capstan, and then led forward via rollers situated under the deckhead of the upper deck. Near the hawse holes the messenger was passed round a vertical roller then led back aft to the capstan.

To weigh the anchor, short light lines termed nippers were passed round both cable and messenger, binding them together. This was done by an able seaman, who passed the nipper over to a ship's boy, who then walked along with the cable as it was hove in, holding the end of the nipper until he reached the hatchway down which the cable passed to the cable tier in the hold. Having removed the nipper at the hatchway, the boy then ran forward with it to the seaman, so that it could be used again to marry the cable to the messenger (and this is where the British term 'nipper' for a small boy had its origin).

The operation is clearly illustrated by the eighteenth-century print accompanying the above detailed account of the system. To the right on the focsle-head can be seen the hooks

Stowing the cable in a ship of the line, anonymous eighteenth-century line and wash drawing. (National Maritime Museum A77)

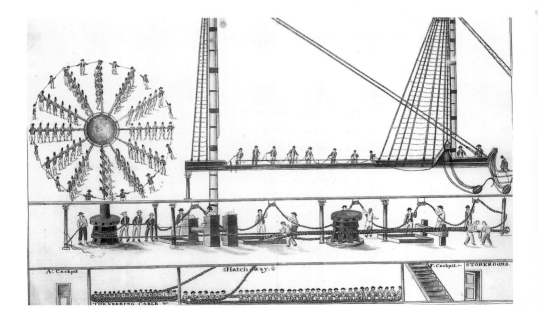

and tackles of the cat and fish davits. On the main deck below are the capstan drum, cable and messenger. The forward capstan, termed the jeer capstan, and the cable bitts are situated between the forward hatch and the seaman passing the nipper. In the hold are the unfortunate seamen stowing the wet and slimy cable. Top left are the Royal Marines and seamen manning the capstan bars, usually encouraged in their long and tedious task by the sound of a fiddle (or possibly sea shanties in merchant ships, which is perhaps the original purpose for such songs). This must have been very necessary, as weighing the anchor might involve heaving in 90 fathom of cable. To make it fast to the cable or riding bitts it was 'stoppered off' by a series of rope stoppers attached to ringbolts on the deck between the manger (formed by a short bulkhead situated abaft the hawse holes) and the cable bitts. When the cable was turned up (*ie* wound as illustrated), the stoppers could be removed and the vessel would be riding on her cable secured to the cable bitts.

The main bowers remained shackled to the cable, with spare bowers stowed in the fore channels astern of them. Smaller anchors might be stowed below, or in the boats, at the beginning of a reasonably long voyage.

Note: The author wishes to make it clear that the description of weighing the anchor is from papers most generously passed on to her by Captain Neville Upham, formerly of the National Maritime Museum, and not from her own research.

A bower anchor, its buoy, and the fish davit on a contemporary model of about 1740. (National Maritime Museum C4564a)

The earliest forms | 1

Stone anchors

Early man presumably secured his craft, whatever form it took, by dragging it on shore as far as possible. But curiosity about the unknown, hopes of a better catch – one or both – led him to deeper waters, where he needed the means of holding his position.

Various writers have considered possible methods which may have been tried. Richard Hakluyt, an Elizabethan clergyman and a scholarly geographer with a passionate belief in England's advancement through overseas exploration, quoted in his collection of eyewitness accounts published about 1600 this method of anchoring: 'To sette with long poles as the distance seemeth', to 'sette' being synonymous in Dutch with 'to anchor'. J W van Nouhuys describes 'long overhanging bows seen in the native canoes of New Guinea, pierced with a vertical hole through which a pole was driven vertically into the river bed, allowing the craft to rise and fall on it with the tide.' In a dugout of the fifth or sixth century recovered near Rotterdam exactly the same method had been used.

Ingenious as these devices were, they had an obvious disadvantage: they were useful only where the craft's owner could wade ashore to a riverbank. This applied equally to the more sophisticated version developed by the Chinese. The solution was the stone anchor; attached to a rope of natural fibres and carried in the craft, it functioned as all anchors have done since. Stone anchors were presumably used wherever the seafarer was prepared to venture. They were and are being found by divers

A simple stone anchor with a single hole for a cable. (National Maritime Museum D5396)

in increasing numbers even in British waters, now that much diving for pleasure has been transformed into serious research, and aided by technical advances in equipment.

A name conspicuous amongst marine archaeologists is that of Honor Frost, not only for her adventurous underwater explorations, but for her classification of the stone anchors she has discovered. She divides them as follows:

1. *Rock anchors.* A simple stone weight anchor which would hold on a rocky seabed, with a single hole pierced for a rope.

2. *Sand anchors.* Flat stones pierced

A more complex form of stone anchor with three holes, two of which may have originally housed sticks to improve holding power on a sandy bottom. (Author)

with holes additional to that for a rope, through which hard, sharpened sticks were thrust, to protrude to equal lengths. These held well in a sandy bottom, and, as far-fetched as it may seem, are the forerunners of the innovative types used to moor present-day oil platforms (see the final chapter). From these stakes were developed arms and flukes.

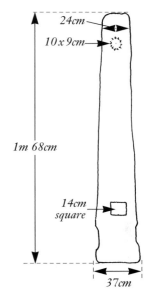

3. *Composite anchors*. A combination of 1 and 2: *eg* a crooked piece of tree root with a stone lashed to it to sink it. It has been suggested that the Chinese Emperor Wu of 2205-2197 BC, who was interested in engineering methods, could lay claim to the invention of this type.

Possible appearance of a stone anchor pierced with sticks. (Author)

Numbers 1 and 2 were roughly flat triangular or rectangular pieces of stone (limestone or sandstone according to that available locally), which gives a clue to their place of origin and that of the craft which carried them. The hole for the rope was in the apex. Their size and weight varied widely and also offers a clue to the size of the vessel concerned.

With reference to type 3 composite anchors, the Curator of the Cyprus Museum, Mr K Nicholoau, in association with Dr H W Catling, Senior Assistant Keeper of the Ashmolean Museum, Cambridge, offered an interesting suggestion when describing three stone anchors found in Larnaka Bay, Larnaka being one of the most important Late Bronze Age settlements in Cyprus. Two of these were close in size, one being 0.78 metres in height, 0.58 metres in width and 0.18 metres in thickness; the other was 0.71 metres in height, 0.64 metres in width and 0.14 in thickness. Both were pierced with three holes, one at the 'top' and two at the 'base', that at the 'top' of one being very roughly square. This led Mr Nicholoau to consider the possibility that the hole was cut for a form of stock, which in turn implies that the larger portion of the stone might be the equivalent of the modern anchor shank in its function. He noted that the site where all three were found was not occupied after the end of the Late Bronze Age.

Drawing of a stone anchor discovered in Raysut harbour, Oman in 1976. (Author)

24cm

10 x 9cm

1m 68cm

14cm square

37cm

Dating the stone anchor has always offered problems. In 1975 an expedition from the Institute of Thracian Studies produced some possible answers while surveying the remains of one of the ports of ancient Apollonia Pontica on the Black Sea. Twenty-three new stone anchors were discovered, sixteen having been used as building material in the substructure of one of

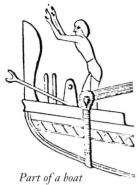

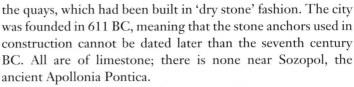

Part of a boat from an Egyptian relief in the tomb of king Sahure relief. The pyramidical object in the bow is thought to be a stone anchor similar to that found at Raysut.

A cut stone anchor recovered from the trireme harbour near Piraeus, Greece. (Hellenic Naval Museum)

the quays, which had been built in 'dry stone' fashion. The city was founded in 611 BC, meaning that the stone anchors used in construction cannot be dated later than the seventh century BC. All are of limestone; there is none near Sozopol, the ancient Apollonia Pontica.

A collection of stone anchors now in the town museum at Sozopol was found lying on a sandy bottom in the sea off the town. A geological survey of the nearby shore concluded that having stabilised at the beginning of the third millenium BC the shore was starting to submerge in the fifth century BC, a process continuing at a minute but constant rate. Thus anchors now found at 8-10 metres depth may actually have lain on the fifth-century coastline, so possibly dating them two centuries earlier than those used in the quay's construction.

Between the fifth and first centuries BC the Apollonian Polis, a politically independent state, acted as intermediary between Thracians and Aegeans. Divers have found stocks of lead anchors only in all ten Apollonian ports. Coins of the same period also found bearing the device of the Polis show on the reverse a composite lead and wood anchor with curved stock, implying that stone anchors were no longer used by trading ships of Apollonia and its partners from the Aegean. Pottery found in association with the coins was of the sixth to the first centuries BC. These results are due to the research in the area of Bojidar Dimitrov and Casimir Nicolov of the Institute of Thracaology, of the Bulgarian Academy of Science of Sofia.

Turning from these complications, not without relief, to the anchors carried by the Greek triremes, one finds a simpler form. This is an elongated stone pyramid, pierced at the apex only from side to side, with one vertical hole there to allow an elaborate knotting of the hawser for extra security. A number were recovered from the Zia Liman, a bay close to Piraeus where the triremes lay at anchor. They are exhibited in the Maritime Museum of Piraeus and the Archaeological Museum of Piraeus.

Killicks

Over the centuries ships braving 'the dangers of the sea and the violence of the enemy', to quote the Naval Prayer, and the anchors they carried, grew in size and changed their form. However, what might be called a subculture of killicks remained unchanging. 'Killick' is the name given to the simple form used by fishermen and early seamen generally in all parts of the world with littoral access. In Europe the name is variously traceable to Breton, Cornish or Norwegian roots (*The New English Dictionary*).

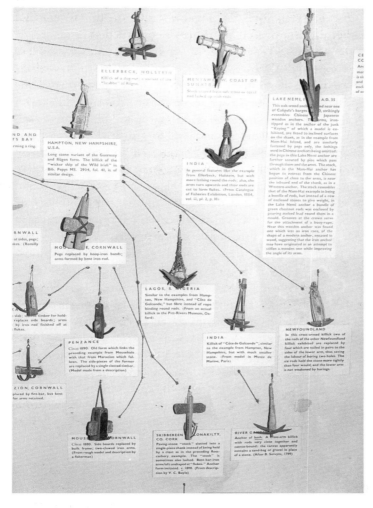

Part of the National Maritime Museum's chart showing the variety and geographical dispersion of killicks. (National Maritime Museum C6754/26)

Examples from the fine collection of models by H H
Brindley, originally in the Museum of Archaeology and
Ethnology in Cambridge and now in the care of the National
Maritime Museum at Greenwich, show a basic type predomi-
nating. This consists of a framework of four, or sometimes six,
supple rods, often willow. One end of these pierce, or are oth-
erwise secured to, a base formed of a crosspiece of thicker and
harder wood, oak where available. The points of this crosspiece
are sharpened to provide a secure grip on the sea bed. At their
other ends the rods are drawn together to complete a 'cage'
holding one or more heavy stones. Here the now-formed
killick is attached to the fisherman's line. As ground tackle it
was easy to handle: it could be broken out of the sea bed and
weighed without difficulty when the user's boat was directly
over it. And being made of 'free' materials it was very
economical.

Variations on this form come from widely spread parts of the
world. One from the River Ganges is a cross-armed killick with
rods bound closely together and the whole canvas-bound, this
apparently containing a sandbag, or gravel in place of one
stone. From Hampton, New Hampshire, a long stone variant
in a killick resembles another from India with a smaller stone.
From Lagos there is one similar, but with fibre binding round
the rods. Of three from Cornwall, one makes use of timber bars
with hoop iron bands as side pieces, and as arms, a bent iron
rod. A single slotted timber with iron arms forms another, and
the third has a built frame instead of side boards, with two-
clawed iron arms. The three all date from the late 1800s. One
from China, naturally more sophisticated, resembles an
umbrella half-opened, its four arms made of oak, iron tipped,
nailed and lashed into position round a central wooden shank
and containing stones.

Generally fishermen from northwest Europe, from New-
foundland and from the Far East, South America and the
Mediterranean all made anchors of stone and wood. While
Breton fishermen used killicks as late as the early l900s, a rock
drawing near Himmelstadlund in Sweden, dated around 1200
BC shows fishing from an open boat, moored with some form
of ground tackle.

Killicks are still seen not only in use, but as symbols, and
appropriately in the Royal Navy. The fouled anchor emblem,

worn on the left sleeve of a Leading Seaman's jumper indicates his rating – the writer wore one with considerable pride – and he is often known as the Killick and addressed as such. On promotion to Petty Officer this badge changes to two fouled anchors crossed diagonally. As before, the question this raises is why the Royal Navy and the shipping world generally settled on the fouled anchor, in practice to be avoided at all costs, as their professional symbol? Known as the 'sailors disgrace', it could only have been the fancy of a landsman.

An example of a typical killick; this version is from Canada.
(National Maritime Museum C6754/15)

2 | *Graeco-Roman anchors*

Stylised representations of the traditional form of anchor seen on ancient Greek coins. Note that some even show a ring at the crown for an anchor buoy line. (National Maritime Museum C7057)

A useful and effective artifact does not change its form and material suddenly. While the town of Ancyra in Egypt was named from the manufacture of stone anchors in its quarries [Stephanus Byzantius, *De Urbibus*, 1688], metal, or metal-and-wood anchors were known at least by 600 BC. Stephanus also wrote: 'Three towns have the name Ancyra, one because once the soldiers of Mithridates there had taken anchors from their enemies.'

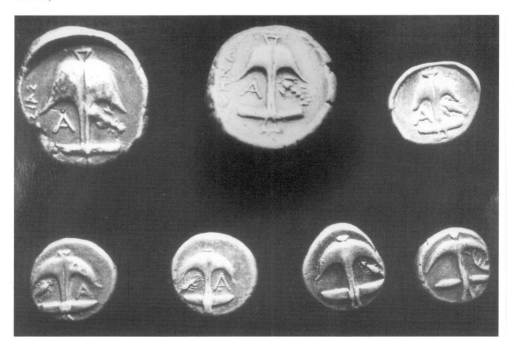

So this artifact now appears to have a name: the Greeks called it *Ancora*, meaning curved or hooked, although a translation of Homer (around 900 BC) gives 'stone for anchor' rather than 'hook'. Sidonis (AD 600) wrote '*Ancora* comes from the Greek . . . like a hand it grips sand or stone.' The Greek Pausanias dismissed stone anchors as 'ancient style' in his *Descriptions of Greece*, referring to Ancura, founded by Midas 'and the anchor found by Midas was still in my time in the temple of Zeus.' His time was around AD 130-180. The Greek poet Theognis, possibly also a seaman, writing about 548-537 BC, was familiar with the anchor's function. 'A young girl is not good for an old man, for she does not follow the rudder as a ship does. She is not held by anchors. She tears the ropes.'

Other, less cynical Greek writers recorded the emergence of iron anchors about the same time, often carried in conjunction with the older wooden type. Strabo (64 BC-AD 25) attributes the invention of the anchor with pairs of arms to Anacharsis (600-590 BC). A last comment on the employment of anchors, from Plutarch: 'A statesman should not, like the last anchor of a ship, lie idle only to wait for the ultimate difficulty and distress of the State.' [From his *Political Sentences*]

The design of these anchors was familiar: from 600-400 BC many coins were stamped with it and showed the ring at the crown of the anchor used to attach a buoy to mark its position and assist its recovery. Almost all showed anchors with noticeably thick arms, and a number were stamped with a device indicating their place of origin as well as the anchor motif. The Curator of Roman coins in the British Museum, Mr Orna Ornstein, kindly identified those illustrated as coins of Apollonia Pontica, a little known city on a small island in the Black Sea (see Chapter 1). The obverse bears the image of Apollo, and the reverse an anchor and lobster. This may indicate the city's reliance on shipping and marine resources.

To increase the anchor's weight, believed to have been only 50-55 pounds, lead or stones were attached to the lower part of the shank to increase it. Large numbers were carried for security against the danger of being caught off a lee shore. St Paul's shipwreck off Malta is described in the Acts of the Apostles, Chapter 27, thus: 'They therefore sounded and found it twenty fathoms, and when they had gone a little further they sounded again and found it fifteen fathoms. Then fearing lest we

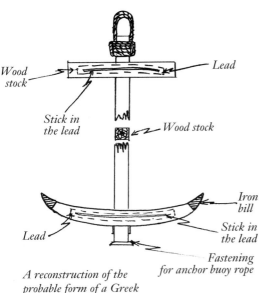

Wood stock — Lead

Stick in the lead — Wood stock

Iron bill

Lead — Stick in the lead

Fastening for anchor buoy rope

A reconstruction of the probable form of a Greek anchor, with lead inserts in stock and arms. (Author)

A Roman wooden anchor. (Author)

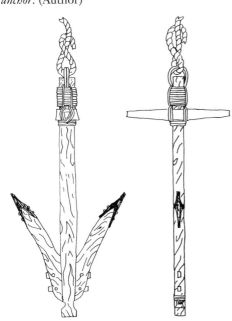

should have fallen upon rocks, they cast four anchors out of the stern and wished for the day' (a feeling only too familiar to many a sailor caught in the same terrifying position). St Paul continues: 'And as the shipmen were about to flee out of the ship, when they had let down the boat into the sea, under colour as though they would have cast anchors out of the foreship . . .'. The last anchor cast was known as the 'sacra' or 'holy' anchor to Roman seafarers, and St Paul's account is interesting also because of the position as well as numbers of anchors and anchor cables carried. Different authorities give varying accounts, from a Roman ship to one of the Athenian navy, but two cables for anchors at the bows and two at the stern for securing the ship to shore seem generally to have been used. According to Cecil Torr, author of *Ancient Ships*, cables of two sizes were used, but precise measurements are unknown. Athenian galleys are recorded as carrying an anchor hung from a beam on either bow.

Somewhere between 316 and 215 BC King Hiero of Syracuse was eager to gain a reputation as a shipbuilder, and built large grain carriers, no doubt to establish his status, much as emerging nations now set up airlines. One ship, supervised by Archimedes and described by 'a certain Moschion' [Herodotus, *Persian Wars*, Vol 3] carried four of wood and eight of iron. While anchor cable was usually rope (see the opinions of Theognis above), occasionally chain was used as a 'forerunner' – where the cable lay on the seabed, and so, likely to chafe against rocks.

While the Romans translated *Anchora* as 'bent' not 'hooked', contemporary

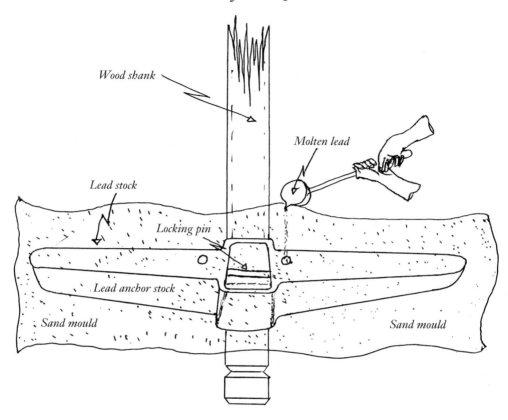

Wood shank

Molten lead

Lead stock

Locking pin

Lead anchor stock

Sand mould

Sand mould

documents suggest that their progress from wooden anchors with lead stocks roughly paralleled that of the Greeks, although the fine mosaic in the Casa di Ancora at Pompeii shows an anchor of the older type with a buoy ring at its crown. These wooden anchors had iron-tipped arms and were necessarily weighted with a stone or lead stock. When stone was used it was merely lashed to the shank, but the lead stock was cast directly on to it. This was done by preparing a sand and clay mould of the form required; the shank was up-ended into this with a hole burnt or drilled into the shank at the position chosen for the stock. Molten lead was then poured into the mould and flowed through the prepared hole in the shank, thus locking stock and shank together. A variety of moulds can be identified from the many lead stocks recovered from British as well as Mediterranean waters: of simple 'box' form, or 'box' form with a further lead bar reinforcement. A lead assembly piece could be cast to strengthen further the junction of arms and

Method of casting a Roman lead stock. (Author)

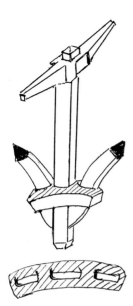

shank; this resulted in arms at an approximate angle of 30 degrees to the shank. Another method was to insert a bar of wood into a gap cut in the shank and the whole was then surrounded by molten lead.

This basic design was inefficient, since the weight being concentrated in the stock allowed the arms to lift from the seabed. As a result, during the first century AD the heavier wooden anchors gradually gave way to iron anchors of pickaxe shape. The latter, possibly originally used as kedges, may be those cast into the sea at St Paul's shipwreck.

Such a lead stock of an anchor, now in the Museum of Wales at Cardiff, is all that remains of a Roman ship lost in the dangerous passage between Bardsey Island and the tip of the Lleyn Peninsula in North Wales. This stock has the bar in the 'box', and, interestingly, the astragals – the knuckle bones used in Roman gambling – cast into it in the form of the winning throw, equivalent of the double six in dice. This fashion, varying with the name of Zeus or of the ship, was developed in the late second century BC and intended to bring good luck to the ship. But fortune was not with this bold little vessel; small, judging from the length (1.18 metres) of her anchor stock, and possibly trying a short cut to or from Chester through the headland's angry seas. Could her 'business in great waters' have had any connection with the tin trade to Britain developing at the same time?

A Roman wooden anchor with a lead 'assembly piece' to strengthen the join between arms and crown. (Author)

A Roman lead stock. (Captain Niksa Seculovic's collection)

With acknowledgments to the National Museum of Wales and 'Notes and News' by George Boon in the *International Journal of Nautical Archaeology*, 6 (1977).

Roman anchors | 3

The Nemi Anchors

Many Roman state sculptures show that rope cables were still used by Roman shipbuilders early in the Christian era, and this was confirmed when Lake Nemi in Italy was drained at the instigation of Mussolini, starting in 1927. The sunken ships thus discovered are assumed to have been used by Caligula, the Roman emperor not exactly famous for a modest lifestyle, for the purposes of pleasure or unorthodox religious rites, in either case safe from critical observation. They are believed to have foundered around AD 40, and with them two anchors, one of the old style and, astonishingly, the other anticipating in its construction anchors forged over 1800 years later.

The latter was found first, sunk in heavy mud, in the position any anchor of its type normally assumes, one arm buried and the stock horizontal. Lieutenant-Commander G C Speziale of the Royal Italian Navy, writing in *The Mariner's Mirror* of 1931, gave a vivid account of his discovery: an iron anchor sheathed in wood, to give a greater bearing surface on a soft sea bed. Its rope cable crumbled as it was touched, but when cleaned it resembled exactly those early designs by Lt Rodger, RN, of about 1830, even to the detachable iron stock secured in position with a cotter pin. As the reader of this account must, Speziale found it extraordinary that so practical a design had lain 'undiscovered' for so many years, even while iron shanks and arms were still matched with heavy wooden stocks. And this appears to be the first recorded instance of a detachable stock in use. The anchor's

The Nemi iron anchor, with wooden sheathing removed. (Author)

An impression of the Nemi iron anchor, as uncovered, with wooden sheathing for extra holding power. (Author)

The more conventional wooden anchor from Lake Nemi; it had a lead stock. (Author)

A small all-lead Roman anchor. (National Maritime Museum D5406)

weight, stamped in one of the arms, was 1275 Roman pounds, roughly 414 kilos.

The second anchor was discovered by following one of several cables indicating the usual mooring areas of the ships. Larger than the first, this was a wooden anchor. Its heavy oak arms were finished with thick iron tips and secured to the shank at an acute angle by pegs with pins which passed through them and the arms. Speziale pointed out also that the lead stock had been cast round a bundle of chestnut rods, and traces of air bubbles formed in the casting were still visible. Uniquely, he found the rope bindings forming the anchor ring, and its cable, were still intact.

Five rope cables were found on the lake bed. Much of them disintegrated to dust when exposed to the air, but not before it was possible to see that the lay of the rope was right-handed, and that they were roughly 15 centimetres in diameter.

The excellent forging of the iron anchor from three pieces of iron bar, one for the shank and one each for the arms, plus one for the stock, suggests the existence of a well-developed forge with a heavy hammer at this period. Relating the Nemi anchors to the eight forged for King Hiero's ships some 250 years earlier (see Chapter 2) offers the possibility of a long-standing anchor-forging industry on a considerable scale. These anchors showed little or no trace of being fitted with flukes, but in the sixth and seventh centuries AD a chisel-shaped fluke on a comparatively lightweight anchor seems to have been used by Byzantine seamen. The wider and fully developed fluke may have begun to appear from AD 300 to 400, but very rarely even then.

With Christianity the anchor became a symbol of hope, but under Rome a method of martyrdom, a somewhat wasteful use of an essential artifact. A sixteenth-century painting by Bernardino Fungai shows the first pope, St Clement, martyred by the Emperor Hadrian

around 100 AD, being cast into the sea with an anchor tied around his neck. The artist included an exquisite depiction of the small temple where the saint's body was discovered with his anchor lying beside him. He is also commemorated in St Clement Danes church, London. At least four saints of the Christian church met the same end: 'One Philomela drowned under the Emperor Diocletian with an anchor tied to her neck.' Even two bishops considered special protectors of seamen were not spared the same fate.

'The Martyrdom of St Clement', by Bernadino Fungai. The ship, and presumably the anchor, is of medieval design. (York City Art Gallery)

While out of chronology here the writer may be excused for describing a similar use of anchors to dispose of those of differing opinions. In Norse literature the story of King Magnus Erlingson, of around AD 1161, runs as follows: 'Erling had Frireck . . . who had inflicted bad wounds on many a bold warrior . . . tied to an anchor and thrown overboard.' Possibly the offender had also failed to observe the first rule for Norse invaders – to pillage first and *then* burn!

The Veneti Anchors

Julius Caesar, sweeping relentlessly across Gaul in 58 BC, reached the peninsula now known as Brittany and was there confronted by the Veneti. Armed with a navy this dominant local tribe – what Henri Waquet writing in 1948 described as a 'true thalassocracy' – monopolised the trade across the Channel with the Britons. Caesar in his account of the *Gallic Wars*, noted that the Veneti anchors were secured by chain not rope cables, unlike the Roman use of the latter. This was borne out by the discovery in Bulbury Camp, one of the many Iron Age hill forts in Dorset, of a Veneti anchor complete with chain cable. This anchor, now handsomely displayed in the Dorchester Museum, has no flukes, but does have a hole pierced at its crown to allow a rope rove through to assist in hoisting it, or mark its position with a buoy. In the same spot, large iron nails as described below were also found.

The same chapter of the *Gallic Wars* went on to describe the construction of the Veneti ships: 'Flatter keels than ours, to deal with shallows and ebb tides for ease in beaching . . . the benches of foot-wide planks, fastened with iron nails as thick as a thumb.' In one struggle with the Roman invaders the Veneti were ill-served by this form of construction: attacked while beached they were unable to retreat to safety as their attackers, supposedly led by the young Brutus, managed to cut their rigging with scythes fastened to long poles. [Henri Waquet] In this connection Roman grapnels, sometimes identified as anchors, had chain cables to prevent their being cut away when grappling with the enemy or burnt by fireships.

The Bulbury anchor and chain cable, of the type used by the Veneti. (Dorset County Museum)

Note: The early account of the Bulbury anchor was in a paper read to the Society of Antiquaries by Edward Cunnington of Dorchester on 30 March 1882.

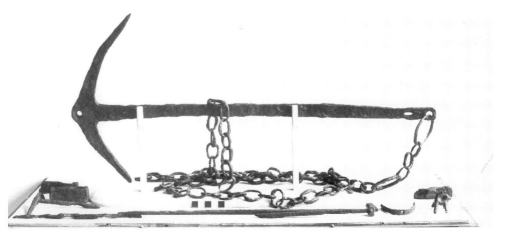

Medieval anchors | 4

Given the paucity of evidence students of this period are rightly cautious in their statements. Roll accounts, illuminated manuscripts and town seals are almost the only way of recognising the medieval anchor, as actual specimens have rarely been positively identified – except for a few Norse or Viking examples from the beginning of the period. Evidence can however be found in the Bayeux Tapestry, at the scene of Harold's arrival in Normandy, and his capture by William's liegeman, count Guido, as he imprudently waded ashore. A seaman, also wading with his skirts well tucked up over bare legs, holds Harold's ship with a turn of the anchor cable round its dragon bows, while astern the bowman of a second ship is about to lower his anchor. Both have the typical curved arms and ring at the crown. Flukes can be seen clear-ly on the second ship, barely on the first, but the latter seems to have one arm of the anchor embedded in the proper position, although the embroiderer could not show the right-angle difference between stock and arms.

Ships appear on the seals of many coastal towns: in those of Portsmouth and Poole, both dating from the late thirteenth

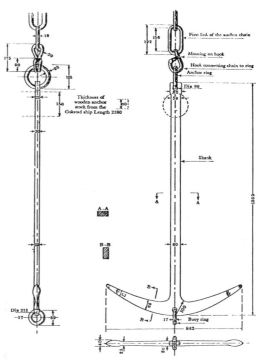

A Viking anchor from the Ladby ship found in Denmark in 1929. Modern research has cast doubt on this reconstruction.
(National Maritime Museum C7052)

The Bayeux tapestry: an anchor is about to be dropped by the bowman of the centre ship. (Author)

century, the anchor is clearly visible. Both have curved arms and the ring at the crown for a buoy rope. The seal of Winchelsea shows the earliest representation of a windlass (early fourteenth century), and in an arrangement similar to

The late thirteenth-century seal of Portsmouth. The anchor at the bow shows a conspicuous ring at the crown. (National Maritime Museum B4900)

The fourteenth-century Winchelsea seal: two men aft are working the windlass, with two others forward handling the cable. (National Maritime Museum B4919)

The seal of Louis de Bourbon, showing the stowed anchor. (National Maritime Museum B4913)

that in the Ladby ship of about AD 950. The anchor, not yet visible, is in process of being weighed by the cable handled, presumably with the aid of the windlass, by two seamen in the bows. The handsome details of the fore and after castles, the trumpeters signalling departure, the splendid shield – all suggest a noble or even royal owner. It possibly represents one of the *Magnae Navis* 'de la Toure' discussed below. One of the finest seals known is that of Louis de Bourbon, Admiral of France from 1436 to 1486. Here is a fully rigged ship, the swelling sail embellished with the fleur-de-lys of France, and an anchor, also with the ring at its crown, shown 'fished', *ie* stowed along the ship's side. (This seal was actually discovered in 1883 in an English shop, being used as a weight.)

Returning briefly to Chapter 3, and the medieval manuscript showing the martyrdom of St Clement, the anchor depicted resembles those seen on the town seals described above, and the ring on the crown is clearly shown. The originals of the anchors on these seals must obviously have been of iron, probably from Sussex or northern Spain, and in the latter case believed to have been shipped as ballast in vessels carrying returning pilgrims from the shrine of St James of Compostella, possibly via Corunna or a nearer port; favourable winds might mean a voyage of about four days. That such a trade existed indicates the growing numbers and increase in welding skills of iron workers.

This writer is much indebted to the painstaking research of Dr Ian Friel, then of the National Maritime Museum, into the building of medieval ships. In a work of this size it is sadly not possible to include all his excellently detailed tables of ships and their dates, anchors and anchor gear, buoys and ropes, but the extracts offered here give a brief account of contemporary ships and the anchors they carried.

The largest type of vessel was the *Magnae Navis* or Great Ship. Where the suffix 'de la Toure' (of the Tower) followed the ship's name, this indicated that she was a King's ship, the royal fleet being based off the Tower of London. For instance, evidence from documents of 1420-1422 refers to the *Holigost de la Toure*, the property of Henry V, who died in the latter year at Vincennes, a *Magnae Navis* having eight anchors, one called 'Marie Tynktawe'. This anchor had been carried in an earlier Great Ship, the *Trinity Royal*, which was apparently partly built of timber and fitments from the *Trinité de la Toure* in 1413. The latter, listed as a *Navis*, smaller than the Great Ships, had four anchors and five pieces of timber bought for anchor stocks, together with iron bands and bars for the capstan, plus six hawsers for buoy ropes. One heavy anchor is recorded as a gift to the *Trinity Royal de la Toure* from Sir John Blount. This ship's building slip was at Greenwich, where the name of the Holy and Undivided Trinity is commemorated in the Trinity Hospital Alms houses for elderly men. Fronting on the Thames, this beautiful building is matched by a splendid dining room, courtyard and gardens.

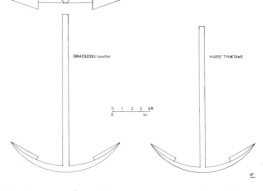

Drawings of the 'Marie Tynktawe' and Grace Dieu *anchor. (Ian Friel)*

Such complicated transfer of materials as well as anchors from old ships to new on the time-honoured principle of cannibalisation seems to have been regular practice at the period. Thus 'Marie Tynktawe' had moved on and 'served' in three ships, leaving behind a tantalising mystery in the origin of her name. This naming of an anchor after a beloved left at home might well enliven the voyages of a VLCC as she wanders from one oil terminal to another, but always far, far away from the chance of any run ashore.

While documentary evidence is almost all that is left of ships of this period, the remains of one, Henry V's Great Ship *Grace Dieu*, built at Southampton in 1418, have actually been seen. A CNA Newsletter of 1968 records the visit of two members to the Hamble River, where she had been burnt in dock at Bursledon in 1439. A very low spring tide uncovered the outline of burnt timber heads as the ebb tide swirled away. Listed as 1400 tons she was the biggest ship of her time, and only a little smaller than Nelson's *Victory*. In 1420 she was recorded as carrying fifteen anchors, including three small ones for the ship's boats. She was also supplied with three cork and five wooden buoys, and various lines, twelve cables and eight thick hawsers, and a mysterious 'apyratus' for hanging anchors during their construction.

Note: A fuller account of the ship can be found in M W Prynne, 'Henry V's *Grace Dieu*', *The Mariner's Mirror* 54 (1968).

5 | *Anchors of the sixteenth and seventeenth centuries*

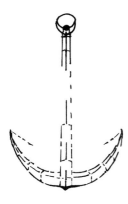

Author's interpretation of the anchor in Matthew Baker's Fragments of Ancient English shipwrightry.

The earliest known contemporary scale drawing of an anchor is in a manuscript called 'Fragments of Ancient English Ship-wrightry', attributed to Matthew Baker (who died in 1613) and preserved in the Pepysian Library at Magdalene College, Cambridge. It shows the curved arm type, and is keyed with letters enabling the reader to follow the accompanying notes on proportions:

'The proportiones of ye best sort of Anckers by L.T.' While it is hardly possible to follow the notes throughout – believed to be in another hand than Baker's – the form of the arms is quite clear. 'The corvinge of ye arme near a circle, but yt is toe rounde. . . ye palme must corve as ye arme doth.' In modern English this would read: 'The curving of the arm is nearly a circle, but it [the circle] is too round. The palm must curve as the arm does.' In other words, it described an ellipse.

The wrought iron anchors recovered from the wreck of the *Mary Rose*, sunk off Portsmouth in 1545 only nine years after a major refit, and only restored to light by the determined efforts of Margaret Rule and her team in 1982, show arms slightly less curved and a longer shank than in Matthew Baker's diagram. They are very similar to those of *La Trinidad Valencera* lost in 1588 after the defeat of the Spanish Armada. Making for home by a route round the north of Scotland, she was one of the three ships wrecked off the Donegal coast of northwest Ireland. A Venetian merchant ship requisitioned in Sicily to convey troops and materials to Spain, she was then 'pressed' into ser-vice as an armed transport, much against the protests of her master, to become one of the largest vessels of the Duke of

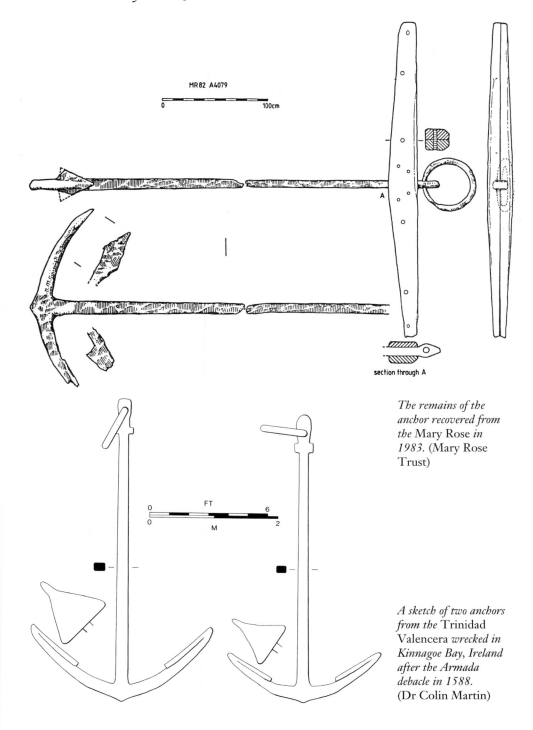

MR 82 A4079

0   100cm

section through A

The remains of the anchor recovered from the Mary Rose *in 1983.* (Mary Rose Trust)

A sketch of two anchors from the Trinidad Valencera *wrecked in Kinnagoe Bay, Ireland after the Armada debacle in 1588.* (Dr Colin Martin)

The remains of an anchor from the Portuguese San Antonio *sunk off Mombasa in 1697.* (Author)

Medina Sidonia's fleet. After the battle 'the winds blew and they were scattered'.

Her voyage ended miserably when she sprang a leak in heavy weather and foundered in Kinnagoe Bay, to the delight of its inhabitants. One survivor reported a mixed reception by the 'wild people', most of whom made the best of a wonderful opportunity for pillage (ancestral Irish portraits, however, suggest that not all receptions were as unfriendly). Guns were believed to have been salvaged earlier on, but it was not until careful exploration of the wreck in 1971 by Dr Colin Martin that two anchors were recovered, the marked 'bill' on the flukes being very noticeable.

An anchor of almost identical type to the above was recently photographed at Fort Jesus, Mombasa. This fort was built by the Portuguese in the late 1500s, and later captured by Arabs from Oman. The anchor is that of the *San Antonio*, built in Bombay in 1680, and sunk by the fort's batteries in 1697 during her attempt to drive out the Arab garrison. It is possible that the anchor as well as the ship that carried it was constructed in Bombay, but it is more likely an import from the West (as late as 1815 British warships built in Bombay were sent home without their structural ironwork, because of the shortage of large-scale metalworking experience locally). Traces of the flukes and the anchor ring remain, although almost destroyed by corrosion. Its proportions would be completely familiar in any English Naval Dockyard of the period.

It was during the period 1540 to 1600 that the gradual change from the curved to the straight-armed anchor appears to have taken place in English vessels, the straight arm proving easier to manufacture in the increasingly large dimensions required by the growth in the size of ships. The angle of arms was at first 40 degrees, later 60. Flukes were an equilateral triangle half the length of the arm, and the shank 4 to 5 fluke-lengths from the crown to the ring end. Following on from Matthew Baker, in the early 1600s a number of printed works containing information on anchors, attributable to known authors, appear for the first time.

A model of an English straight-armed anchor of about 1600, a form that with minor variations was to survive for two hundred years. (National Maritime Museum C8821)

Number and Weight of Anchors, 1602-1640

Ships' tonnage	Total carried 1602	Total carried 1640	Total weights, cwts 1602	Total weights, cwts 1640	Estimated sheet cwts 1602	Actual weights, cwts, 1640: Sheet	1st bower	2nd bower	3rd bower	4th bower	Stream	Kedge
To 100	3	3	13½	10½	—	4	3½	3	—	—	—	—
	to 4	to 5	to 16	to 17¼		to 5½	to 5¼	to 5	5	—	—	1½
101–150	—	5	—	17¼	—	5½	5¼	5	5	—	—	1½
151–200	4	5	28½	34	9	10	9	7	5½	—	—	2½
201–250	4	—	33	—	—	—	—	—	—	—	—	—
251–300	4	7	40¼	76½	13	15	14	14	13	13	5	2½
301–350	4	6	53	58	—	13½	12½	11¾	11¼	—	6½	2½
	to 5	to 7	to 65¼	to 76½		to 15	to 14	to 14	to 13	13	to 5	2½
351–400	—	—	—	—	—	—	—	—	—	—	—	—
401–450	5	—	63¼	—	—	—	—	—	—	—	—	—
	to 6		to 85¾									
451–500	6	7	80½	100½	20	20	19	18	17	17	7	2½
501–550	6	7	82	100½	20	20	19	18	17	17	7	2½
				to 117½			to 24	to 21	to 21	to 20	to 9	2½
551–600	6	7	85¾	100½	—	20	19	18	17	17	7	2½
	to 7		to 116	to 117½		to 24	to 21	to 21	to 20	to 20	to 9	2½
601–650	7	7	116	133½	22¼	25	24	24	23	23	10	3½
				to 144½		to 28	to 26	to 26	to 25	to 25	to 11	3½
651–700	7	—	113½	—	—	—	—	—	—	—	—	—
			to 120½									
701–750	—	7	—	144½	—	28	26	26	25	25	11	3½
751–800	7	7	128½	144½	24½	28	26	26	25	25	11	3½
				to 149		28	to 27	to 27	to 26	to 26	11	4
801–850	—	7	—	144½	—	28	26	26	25	25	11	3½
851–900	7	7	134	144½	26	28	26	26	25	25	11	3½
901–950	7	7	136½	156	26¼	30	28	28	27	27	12	4
951–1000	7	—	134	—	—	—	—	—	—	—	—	—
Prince 1187	—	10	—	214	—	32(2)	30	30	28	28	13 (2)	4 (2)
Sovereign 1522	—	8	—	226	—	55	44	40	36	25	16+8	4+8

Compiled by J T Tinniswood, *The Mariner's Mirror* XXXI (1945).

Continental anchors | 6

In a survey of so down to earth a subject as anchors it may seem frivolous to relate their designs to national characteristics; but this comparison is not entirely invalid.

Dutch Anchors

The Dutch may fairly claim to be the first to specify in print the type and size of anchors appropriate to be carried in various types of vessels. Two Dutch writers, Witsen in 1671 and van Yk in 1697, state that Dutch men-of-war were furnished with four different types, varying in size and strength. The heaviest,

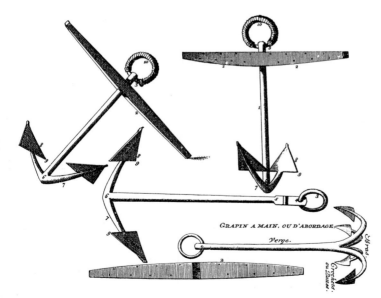

GRAPIN A MAIN, OU D'ABORDAGE.

Verge.

Crochets, ou Pates.

Dutch anchor of the late seventeenth century; note that the wooden stock is secured with nails rather than iron bands. Although taken from a French-language book published in Amsterdam in 1719, it draws heavily on the works of Witsen (1671) and van Yk (1697), so represents earlier Dutch practice. (From David Mortier's L'Art de Batir les Vaisseaux, *1719)*

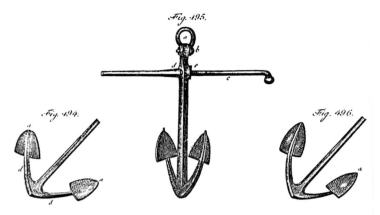

the sheet anchor, was kept ready for an emergency; for normal 'every day' use, there was an anchor ⅞ths of the sheet anchor in weight, and two anchors for use in rivers or inlets. These, the stream and kedge anchors, were ⅞ths of the 'every day' anchor in size.

Dutch anchors must have been strong and solid, since a dour Dutch comment on Spanish anchors, notorious for thinness of metal, at least in the seventeenth century, was the simile 'as meagre as a Spanish anchor'. This may have been due to technical inability in forging them.

The Dutch had a practical rule of thumb for obtaining anchor sizes: briefly, by cubing the number of feet in the anchor's length its weight is obtained. To relate it to the size of ship carrying it, the length of the shank of the anchor is ⅖ths of

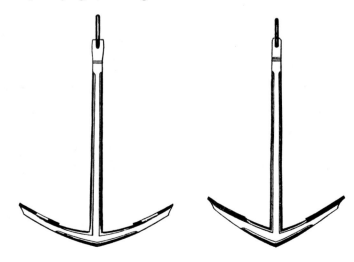

the beam of the ship. Until the introduction of steam in the Dutch navy the formula reads: weight of the anchor in kilos equals the number of guns multiplied by 50. In very large ships the weight of the anchor would be a few kilos lighter than this rule indicates.

Illustrations of Dutch anchors are somewhat confusing: Richard Pering's drawing of a Dutch type has longer arms welded to the shank at a wider angle than those of the French. The palms can only be seen in profile but their length appears exactly the same as those of the latter.

French anchor of about 1760; note the foundry mark on the crown. (From Diderot's Encylopédie, 1751-1772)

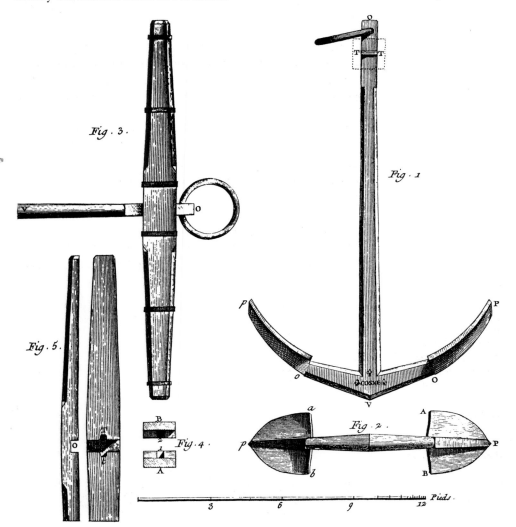

Turning to Pieter le Comte's book *Praktikale Zeevaartkunde* of 1842, the illustrations show a much more decorative type of anchor, with marked curves of the arms towards the shank, nearly half way up the latter. A drawing of a single-fluked mooring anchor is prettified with elegant protrusions on the back of shank and fluke, and an elegantly curving palm. The first mentioned anchor shows, interestingly, a moveable stock with forelock securing its position through the head of the anchor when in use, but a ball at the other end of a curve enabling it to lie safely alongside the shank when stowed.

French Anchors

Researching through drawings of the French anchor of the late eighteenth century the impression is of a decorative form compared with the plain sturdiness of the English Old Admiralty Longshank. In proportions they are very similar, but in detail entirely different.

The shank, which is six-sided, tapers to the junction with the stock. The latter, in two halves like the English, has a marked upward curve from the centre and is held by bands. Judging again from the drawing, these appear to be reinforced by nails.

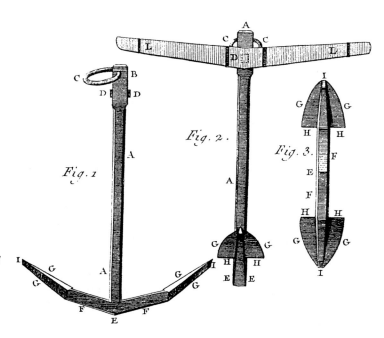

Another French anchor from Diderot, this model with the common upturned stock and palms angled to the arms.

The arms, welded at a more acute angle than the English equivalent, appear shorter. They join the crown in a way very satisfying to the eye. The anchor was marked on the crown with its weight in *livres* (equivalent to 1.08 English pounds), and with a maker's mark on the reverse side together with three fleurs-de-lis.

According to William Burney's *Marine Dictionary* of 1815 (a revised edition of the 1769 original by Falconer), the sheet anchor was termed *la grande ancre*, or, very appropriately, *l'ancre de misericorde*. The best bower was *la seconde ancre*, the small bower *l'ancre d'affourche*. The stream anchor was *l'ancre à empeneller* and the kedge, *l'ancre de touée*. For reference the shank, stock, arms, flukes, crown, ring and palms were *la verge*, *le jât*, *les bras*, *les oreilles*, *le collet* and *les pattes* respectively.

The anchors of a 74-gun ship of the late eighteenth century would be similar to those of the Royal Navy, the sheet being about 16 feet in length, and 5200 pounds in weight. The best bower of the same weight, but 15 feet 8 inches in length. A smaller anchor, *l'ancre à jet* (cast anchor) weighing 1700 pounds was usually carried on board, together with a smaller one weighing about 100 pounds less.

Spanish Anchors

The anchors of *La Trinidad Valencera* have been considered in an earlier chapter, but it is possible that they may not have been Spanish; as she was a Venetian vessel requisitioned in Sicily, they may have been of Italian origin.

Spanish anchors and their forging appear in plates from *The Diccionario de Arquitectura Naval* of 1719-1756, by the Marques de la Victoria, Capitan General de la Real Armada. In the plate 'Ancras Y Boyas' shapes of the anchor are shown, and judging by these the gracefully curving arms were preferred. In one detail the crown of the anchor appears almost to recede between the curve of the arms. This marked curve brings the flukes back within the length of the stock as shown. The flukes resemble nothing so much as a barbed fish hook, which cannot have made the anchor easier to handle. It is interesting to note that the stocks do not have the pronounced upward curve of their French counterparts, but are almost straight on top, though tapered underneath like their English equivalents. Obviously in two halves, they are held by four bands, two to

Small Spanish iron-stocked anchor recovered from Port Mahon, Menorca. (By courtesy of Kin Walker)

each side of the crown reinforced by nails at the outer ends and near the shank. A single-fluke mooring anchor is included, showing the same fearsome palm. All the anchors have wooden stocks; it has been suggested that iron stocks were used as late as the thirteenth century, but disappeared thereafter.

The print also shows buoys, apparently one to each anchor, in case the anchor had to be slipped, and to show its position when the tide turned to avoid its being fouled. Navigational buoys are represented, as is a sea-anchor or drogue to assist in riding out a gale: it appears to be a bucket made of canvas.

The Old Admiralty Longshank anchor | 7

The number of anchors appropriate to the size of ship appears to have been accepted from at least classical times. Handling them without the later inventions of capstan and windlass limited their size, and the numerous small anchors carried as already noted suited the craft of the earlier period. No artifact of long standing changes its form and discards the old at a given

A bower anchor thought to come from the 90-gun three-decker Association, *Sir Cloudesley Shovell's flagship wrecked off the Scilly Isles in 1707.* (F E Gibson)

moment, but as ships increased in size the many small anchors were replaced by fewer and larger versions. By 1800 a First Rate of 100 guns probably carried seven anchors; two hundred years earlier, the largest warship probably eleven.

Early Types and Proportions

Two seamen of the early seventeenth century recorded their views on the types and proportions of anchors. Sir Henry Mainwaring in his *Seaman's Dictionary* of 1622 stated that the shank is twice as long as one of the flukes, plus half the beam (this, the beam, being assumed to be the distance between the tips of the flukes). The anchor stock was roughly the same length as the shank. The flukes were generally the shape of

The National Maritime Museum's example of an old Admiralty Longshank anchor. (Dr David Nuttall)

equilateral triangles and half the length of the arm, the anchor ring being slightly less than the fluke in 'diameter'.

Captain John Smith, famous for his exploration of the territory that was to become Virginia, and his rescue from death by the Princess Pocahontas, wrote *A Sea Grammar* in 1627 detailing types and uses of anchors to be carried, as follows:

The *Kedger*, the smallest, was used for working the ship up or down a river or a narrow inlet; this anchor would be carried in one of the ship's boats at the end of a long cable. At a given distance it would be lowered over the boat's side, when the ship's capstan, if any, would be used to haul on the cable and draw the vessel to the chosen anchorage. The process could be repeated to work the ship higher upstream. The *Stream* anchor was slightly larger and used to stem an easy stream. The *Bower*, so called from the position where it was carried, was the largest. The complement was usually two kedgers, one stream and four bowers until the end of the nineteenth century, when the so-called sheet anchor was discarded, and two bowers and a spare bower were carried.

The strongest of the bowers, at first called the sheet or best bower anchor, was carried on the starboard side of the ship to make the most of the weather cycles. First the port bower was let go, then as the wind increased the sheet anchor was let go, and both cables paid out. As the wind in the northern hemisphere tends to shift from southwest to northwest, when the wind veered both cables would still lie out ahead of the ship. Had the reverse procedure with the anchors been adopted (*ie* the starboard bower let go first), the cables would have crossed as the wind shifted to the northwest, causing potential knots – known to those of a seafaring bent as a 'snake's honeymoon'.

Recorded as holding well, the Old Admiralty Longshank anchor continued to be the standard pattern during the eighteenth century. Its one great fault was a tendency for the arms to break off at the crown when heavily stressed. This was the result of shortcomings in the manufacture since the hammers of the time were incapable of expelling all the air bubbles during welding, leaving potential weak spots when the iron cooled.

The Eighteenth Century

This century produced for the first time an extensive English language survey of naval architecture, shipbuilding, rigging and other aspects of the craft in *Britain's Glory, or Ship-Building Unvail'd*. This was the work of William Sutherland, published in 1717, and followed *The Shipbuilder's Assistant*, a smaller work he published in 1711.

He was then employed as a 'Quarter-man' (a senior shipwright with responsibility over a 'gang' of workmen) in Deptford Dockyard, but through the patronage of the Earl of Sutherland he became Master Caulker at Sheerness in 1717. This appointment was confirmed in 1727, the year of George II's accession, and he died eleven years later.

This book is probably the first to give an account of the types of anchors in use since the previous century, and it is interest-

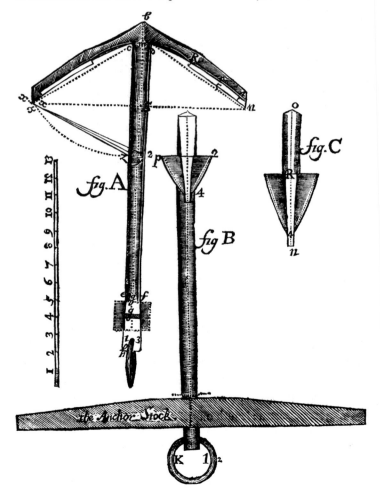

The drawing of an Admiralty anchor in William Sutherland's Ship-Building Unvail'd *of 1717.* (National Maritime Museum C6997/6)

In the next Place I shall shew the particular Shape and Dimensions of the Anchors, observing that it's general, for the length of the Shank of the biggest Anchor, in any Ship, to be $\frac{2}{5}$ of the Ships extream breadth.

Tunnage of the Six Sizes	1677 Tuns		1488 Tuns		969 Tuns		625 Tuns		364 Tuns		225 Tuns	
Weight of the biggest Anchor	*C. qr. l.* 71 : 2 : 0		*C. qr. l.* 64 : 0 : 0		*C. qr. l.* 45 : 0 : 0		*C. qr. l.* 30 : 0 : 0		*C. qr. l.* 18 : 3 : 6		*C. qr. l.* 11 : 2 : 1	
Cube Root of the Weight	4—$\frac{7}{100}$		4		3—$\frac{53}{100}$		3—$\frac{1}{10}$		2—$\frac{65}{100}$		2—$\frac{26}{100}$	
	feet	*Inch.*	*feet*	*Inch.*	*feet*	*Inch.*	*feet*	*Inch.*	*feet*	*Inch*	*feet*	*Inch.*
Length of the Shank as aforesaid	18	6	18	2	16	1	14	2	12	2	10	8
Bigness of the great End of ditto	0	$11\frac{1}{2}$	0	$11\frac{1}{10}$	0	$10\frac{1}{10}$	0	$8\frac{8}{10}$	0	$7\frac{11}{20}$		$6\frac{14}{20}$
Ditto at the small end	0	$8\frac{13}{20}$	0	$8\frac{5}{10}$	0	$7\frac{1}{8}$	0	$6\frac{6}{10}$	0	$5\frac{13}{20}$	0	$4\frac{7}{10}$
Length of the Square	2	11	2	$10\frac{4}{10}$	2	$6\frac{4}{10}$	2	3	1	11	1	8
Length to the Nut	1	11	1	$10\frac{6}{10}$	1	$8\frac{8}{10}$	1	$5\frac{6}{10}$	1	$3\frac{1}{10}$	1	$1\frac{4}{10}$
Bigness of the Nut Square	0	$2\frac{3}{10}$	0	$2\frac{26}{100}$	0	2	0	$1\frac{76}{100}$	0	$1\frac{51}{100}$	0	$1\frac{14}{100}$
Diamiter of the Rings inside clear	2	$1\frac{1}{2}$	2	1	1	10	1	$7\frac{6}{10}$	1	3	1	2
Bigness of the Ring	0	4	0	$3\frac{24}{100}$	0	$3\frac{48}{100}$	0	$3\frac{6}{100}$	0	3	0	$2\frac{71}{100}$
Diameter of the Hole for the Ring	0	$4\frac{6}{10}$	0	$4\frac{5}{10}$	0	$3\frac{98}{100}$	0	$3\frac{5}{10}$	0	3	0	$2\frac{66}{100}$
Length of the Crown	1	2	1	$1\frac{7}{10}$	0	$11\frac{1}{10}$	0	$9\frac{3}{4}$	0	$8\frac{7}{20}$	0	$7\frac{7}{10}$
Length of the Arm	7	0	6	9	6	1	5	$0\frac{7}{20}$	4	$0\frac{6}{10}$	4	$0\frac{1}{20}$
Breadth of the Flook	2	8	2	$7\frac{5}{10}$	2	$3\frac{8}{10}$	2	$0\frac{4}{10}$	1	9	1	6
Length of ditto	3	9	3	$8\frac{1}{3}$	3	$3\frac{2}{10}$	2	$10\frac{4}{10}$	2	$5\frac{5}{10}$	2	2
Thickness of ditto	0	$2\frac{9}{10}$	0	$2\frac{85}{100}$	0	$2\frac{51}{100}$	0	$2\frac{22}{100}$	0	$1\frac{9}{10}$	0	$1\frac{68}{100}$
Square of the Arm at the Flook	0	7	0	$6\frac{9}{10}$	0	$6\frac{1}{10}$	0	$5\frac{7}{10}$	0	$4\frac{6}{10}$	0	$4\frac{1}{20}$
Length of the Bill	0	$10\frac{1}{2}$	0	$10\frac{3}{10}$	0	$9\frac{1}{10}$	0	8 0	0	$6\frac{9}{10}$	0	$6\frac{1}{10}$
Rounding of the Flook	0	$1\frac{16}{100}$	0	$1\frac{14}{100}$	0	$1\frac{1}{10}$	0	$0\frac{89}{100}$	0	$0\frac{76}{100}$	0	$0\frac{66}{100}$
Clutching of the Arm	3	6	3	$5\frac{1}{3}$	3	$0\frac{4}{10}$	2	6	2	$4\frac{5}{10}$	2	$1\frac{2}{10}$
Inside meeting	6	6										
Outside meeting	6	6										
Middle meeting	6	6										

Table of dimensions of Admiralty anchors for six rates of ship, from Sutherland's Ship-Building Unvail'd *of 1717.* (National Maritime Museum C6997/9)

ing to note that he also recommended that arms should be curved, to lessen the sheering movement as the anchor is broken out of the ground when weighing. As already noted, after the mid-sixteenth century with the need for larger anchors, straight-armed anchors appear to have been introduced to English vessels, but this work suggests a continuing preference for curved arms.

Sutherland illustrates his book with extensive tables. Prefacing one he writes, 'I shall shew the particular Shape and Dimensions of the Anchor, observing that it's general for the length of the Shank of the biggest Anchor, in any Ship, to be 2⁄5 of the Ship's extreme breadth.' Anchor weights appropriate to the tonnage of six ships, from 1677 'tuns' down to 225 are given, and equally importantly, they show the measurements of anchors and their constituent parts relative to each ship's size.

However, if the data is supposed to relate to the Navy's six formal Rates then the quoted tonnages imply a reference to the practice of the late seventeenth century, rather than the date of

A small iron-stocked kedge anchor from the grounding of Cook's Adventure *at Tahiti in 1773. It weighs 480 kilos or about 9¹/₂ hundredweight in traditional units.* (Museum of Shipwrecks, Bay of Islands, New Zealand)

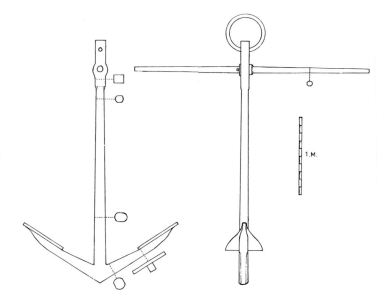

1.M.

publication. Another and significant table, considering the corruption supposedly rife in dockyards, gives 'The whole value of materials and workmanship, or the charge for the anchor delivered from the forge for the biggest Size.' And a further table relates to the weight of coals required to forge the anchor according to its size. Costs of making the anchor were calculated on wages for the number of men involved, usually twelve, one being the Foreman – and not omitting the charge for a gallon of beer supplied daily.

Sutherland includes a survey of the current various opinions on the angles of arms to shanks, and importantly, comments on the desirability of testing anchors to prove correct manufacture. For safety in a gale he proposed a long scope of cable – up to three lengths joined end to end, and this long catenary is still considered necessary to the holding powers of an an anchor (see Introduction). Sutherland's precise and beautiful drawing of an Old Admiralty Longshank Bower anchor shows its exact proportions, with arms hardly curved in spite of his recommendations. Notice that the 'Bill' on the fluke has markedly increased, and is similar to those tipping the flukes of the anchors from *La Trinidad Valencera*.

The term 'Establishment' may be considered to express the number of ships required to carry out the tasks imposed by the

Board of Admiralty's political masters, together with all the necessities for operations in home or foreign waters. From this was derived the notion of standardised fittings and stores for each class of vessel. Tables were drawn up giving details of these necessities in every category. In 1763 the size and weights of anchors and cables appropriate to each class were laid down in the accompanying table.

By the end of the eighteenth century and according to an unknown source the Masters of merchantmen were supposedly awarded £5 by the insurance underwriters if they used the sheet anchor to save the ship from going ashore. But since the mer-

An Admiralty anchor discovered at Norfolk Island, New South Wales. It is believed to be a bower from HMS Sirius, the ex-merchant vessel purchased as flagship of the 'First Fleet' to Australia. Classed as a Sixth Rate in Royal Navy service, she was wrecked off Norfolk Island in 1790. This photograph demonstrates the large size of anchor required even by a relatively modest ship of 511 tons. (National Maritime Museum B1717)

56   Anchors

The Established Sizes and Weights of Anchors for the Royal Navy, c1763

	Number and Weight of the different Anchors to each Ship			Dimensions of the Anchors, in Feet and Inches										Number and Weight of the different Cables to each Ship: With the number of Yarns in each Strand						
	No.	Cwt	Qrs	lb	L	S	T	T	L	P	B	P	T	P	N	S	W				N of Y
100 Guns																					
Bowers	5	81	0	0	19	2	0	9½	3	3¾	3	2¼	0	3¼	9	24	120	3	3	0	334
Stream	1	21	0	0	13	4	0	5¼	2	0¼	1	11⅜	0	1¼	1	15	46	3	14	8	130
Kedge	1	10	2	0	10	4	0	4½	1	8¹¹⁄₁₆	1	9⁹⁄₁₆	0	1¼	–	–	–	–	–	–	–
90 Guns																					
Bowers	5	73	0	0	18	7	0	8⅞	3	1¼	3	0¼	full	3	9	23	106	0	27	8	308
Stream	1	18	0	0	12	10	0	5⅛	1	10½	1	11¼	full	1⅝	1	14½	43	3	5	15	122
Kedge	1	9	0	0	9	9	0	4	1	7	1	8¼	full	1⅛	–	–	–	–	–	–	–
74 Guns																					
Bowers	4	67	0	0	18	1	0	8½	3	0¼	2	10¾	0	2⅞	7	22	100	2	19	6	285
Stream	1	16	0	0	12	2	0	4⅞	1	9⅞	1	11¼	0	1⅝	1	13½	37	3	24	8	106
Kedge	1	8	0	0	9	6	0	3¼	1	6	1	7⅛	full	1⅛	–	–	–	–	–	–	–
64 Guns																					
Bowers	4	57	0	0	17	3	0	8	2	9¼	2	8¼	0	2⅜	7	21	91	3	14	0	255
Stream	1	15	0	0	11	10	0	4¾	1	9¼	1	11	0	1⅝	1	13	35	0	23	5	98
Kedge	1	7	2	0	9	4½	0	3¹¹⁄₁₆	1	5½	1	6½	full	1⅛	–	–	–	–	–	–	–
50 Guns																					
Bowers	4	49	0	0	16	7	0	7⅝	2	8¼	2	6¼	0	2⁷⁄₁₆	7	19	73	0	23	6	209
Stream	1	11	0	0	10	6	0	4⅛	1	8⅛	1	9⅜	0	1¼	1	12	30	0	0	0	83
Kedge	1	5	2	0	8	6	0	3⁵⁄₁₆	1	3½	1	4½	0	1⅛	–	–	–	–	–	–	–
44 Guns																					
Bowers	4	40	0	0	15	10	0	7¼	2	5½	2	4½	0	2¼	7	17½	63	3	5	14	177
Stream	1	10	0	0	10	2	0	4⅛	1	8	1	9½	0	1¼	1	12	30	0	0	0	83
Kedge	1	5	0	0	8	3	0	3¼	1	3	1	4	0	1⅛	–	–	–	–	–	–	–
32 Guns																					
Bowers	4	33	0	0	15	3	0	6¹⁵⁄₁₆	2	3¼	2	2½	full	2¹⁄₁₆	7	16½	56	2	24	8	157
Stream	1	8	1	0	9	6	0	3¾	1	6	1	7⅛	0	1⅛	1	9½	18	3	5	14	52
Kedge	1	4	0	0	7	9	0	3⅛	1	2	1	3	0	1	–	–	–	–	–	–	–
28 Guns																					
Bowers	4	31	0	0	15	0	0	6¹⁵⁄₁₆	2	3¼	2	2½	full	2¹⁄₁₆	6	16	53	1	9	6	148
Stream	1	8	0	0	9	6	0	3¾	1	6	1	7⅛	0	1⅛	1	9	16	3	14	0	47
Kedge	1	4	0	0	7	9	0	3⅛	1	2	1	3	0	1	–	–	–	–	–	–	–
20 Guns																					
Bowers	4	25	0	0	14	0	0	6¼	2	1½	2	0	0	1⅞	6	14½	43	3	5	15	122
Stream	1	7	2	0	9	4½	0	3¹¹⁄₁₆	1	5½	1	6½	0	1¼	1	7½	11	2	24	8	32
Kedge	1	3	2	0	7	6	0	3	1	1½	1	2½	0¹⁵⁄₁₆		–	–	–	–	–	–	–
14 Guns																					
Bowers	3	20	2	0	13	3	0	5¹¹⁄₁₆	2	0⅛	1	11¹¹⁄₁₆	0	1¼	5	13½	37	3	24	8	106
Stream	1	7	0	0	9	3	0	3⅜	1	5	1	6	0	1⅛	1	7½	11	2	24	8	32
Kedge	1	3	2	0	7	6	0	3	1	1½	1	2½	0¹⁵⁄₁₆		–	–	–	–	–	–	–

First and Second Rate Ships generally have (beside the undermentioned) another smaller Kedge, of about 4½ or 5 cwt with them.

CONTRACTIONS EXPLAINED.
L S: *Length of the Shank.* T T: *Thickness of the Trent.*
L P: *Length of the Palms.* B P: *Breadth of the Palms.*
T P: *Thickness of the Palms.*

N.B. The Diameter of each Ring, from the Outside to Outside, is the Breadth of its respective Palms: And the Size of the Ring is Half the Size of the Small of the Round of the Shank.

CONTRACTIONS EXPLAINED.
N: *Number of Cables of the same size*
S: *Size of the Cables.*
W: *Weight of each Cable at 100 fathoms.*
N of Y: *Number of Yarns in each Strand.*

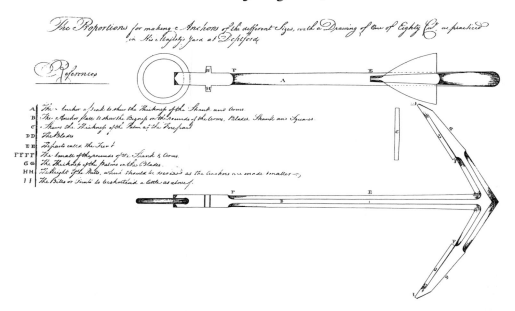

The Proportions for making Anchors of the different Sizes, with a Drawing of One of Eighty C.wt as practised in His Majesty's Yard at Deptford

References

A	This Anchor is made to shew the Thickness of the Shank and Arms
B	The Anchor plate to shew the Bigness on the Rounds of the Arms, Blades, Shank and Squares
C	Shews the Thickness of the Palm at the Forepart
DD	The Blades
EE	The parts called the Ears
FFFF	The small of the rounds of the Shank & Arms
GG	The Thickness of the Palms in the Blades
HH	The height of the Nuts, which should be lessened as the Anchors are made smaller
II	The Bills or points to be shortened a little as above

chant service was far less regulated than the Navy, there are no known tables of anchor sizes that apply. The earliest recorded suggestion of such standardisation is contained in Peter Hedderwick's *Practice of Shipbuilding*. Although not published until 1830, so apparently ineligible for inclusion in this chapter, his table of anchor sizes and cables for merchant ships of 10 to 1300 tons shows that not only the Board of Admiralty considered established relations between the ship and its fittings to be a good thing.

An official Royal Navy drawing from the Deptford Dockyard Master Shipwright's office of an 80 hundredweight anchor, about 1790. It is accompanied by a table of dimensions for anchors of every weight from 1 to 80 hundredweight. (From Public Records Office Adm 106/3322)

100 Guns, and upwards.

Anchors.	No. allowed.	Weight of each. (Cwt.)	Total Weight. (Cwt.)	Rate per Cwt. (£ s. d.)	Value. (£ s. d.)
Bower ..	4	90	360	4 12 4½	1662 15 0
Stream ..	1	21		2 8 3½	50 14 1½
Kedge ..	1	10½			
Ditto ..	1	5		2 7 3	36 12 4½

100 Guns.

Anchors.	No. allowed.	Weight of each. (Cwt.)	Total Weight. (Cwt.)	Rate per Cwt. (£ s. d.)	Value. (£ s. d.)
Bower ..	4	84	336	4 12 4½	1551 18 0
Stream ..	1	21		2 8 3½	50 14 1½
Kedge ..	1	10½			
Ditto ..	1	5		2 7 3	36 12 4½

98 or 90, 2050 Tons or upwards.

Anchors.	No. allowed.	Weight of each. (Cwt.)	Total Weight. (Cwt.)	Rate per Cwt. (£ s. d.)	Value. (£ s. d.)
Bower ..	4	84	336	4 12 4½	1551 18 0
Stream ..	1	21		2 8 3½	50 14 1½
Kedge ..	1	10½			
Ditto ..	1	5		2 7 3	36 12 4½

98 or 90, under 2050 Tons.

Anchors.	No. allowed.	Weight of each. (Cwt.)	Total Weight. (Cwt.)	Rate per Cwt. (£ s. d.)	Value. (£ s. d.)
Bower ..	4	76	304	4 12 4½	1450 5 9
Stream ..	1	18			
Kedge ..	1	9		2 7 3	74 8 4
Ditto ..	1	4½			

80 Guns.

Anchors.	No. allowed.	Weight of each. (Cwt.)	Total Weight. (Cwt.)	Rate per Cwt. (£ s. d.)	Value. (£ s. d.)
Bower ..	4	76	304	4 12 4	1450 5 9
Stream ..	1	18			
Kedge ..	1	9		2 7 3	74 8 4½
Ditto ..	1	4½			

74 Guns, 1799 Tons and upwards.

Anchors.	No. allowed.	Weight of each. (Cwt.)	Total Weight. (Cwt.)	Rate per Cwt. (£ s. d.)	Value. (£ s. d.)
Bower ..	4	73	292	4 4 6½	1231 6 2½
Stream ..	1	17½		2 7 3	61 8 6
Kedge ..	1	8½			

74 Guns, under 1799 Tons.

Anchors.	No. allowed.	Weight of each. (Cwt.)	Total Weight. (Cwt.)	Rate per Cwt. (£ s. d.)	Value. (£ s. d.)
Bower ..	4	70	280	4 1 6	1141 0 0
Stream ..	1	17½		2 7 3	61 8 6
Kedge ..	1	8½			

74 Guns, 1740 to 1798 Tons.

Anchors.	No. allowed.	Weight of each. (Cwt.)	Total Weight. (Cwt.)	Rate per Cwt. (£ s. d.)	Value. (£ s. d.)
Bower ..	4	67	268	4 1 6	1092 2 0
Stream ..	1	16		2 7 3	56 14 0
Kedge ..	1	8			

64 Guns.

Anchors.	No. allowed.	Weight of each. (Cwt.)	Total Weight. (Cwt.)	Rate per Cwt. (£ s. d.)	Value. (£ s. d.)
Bower ..	4	57	228	3 8 6	780 18 0
Stream ..	1	15		2 7 3	53 3 1½
Kedge ..	1	7½			

50 Guns, of 1100 Tons.

Anchors.	No. allowed.	Weight of each. (Cwt.)	Total Weight. (Cwt.)	Rate per Cwt. (£ s. d.)	Value. (£ s. d.)
Bower ..	4	52	208	3 4 9¼	706 0 0½
Stream ..	1	11		2 7 3	38 19 7
Kedge ..	1	5½			

50 Guns, under 1100 Tons.

Anchors.	No. allowed.	Weight of each. (Cwt.)	Total Weight. (Cwt.)	Rate per Cwt. (£ s. d.)	Value. (£ s. d.)
Bower ..	4	49	196	3 1 5	601 17 8
Stream ..	1	11		2 7 3	33 19 7½
Kedge ..	1	5½			

44 Guns.

Anchors.	No. allowed.	Weight of each. (Cwt.)	Total Weight. (Cwt.)	Rate per Cwt. (£ s. d.)	Value. (£ s. d.)
Bower ..	4	44	176	2 17 2½	503 8 8
Stream ..	1	10		2 7 3	35 8 9
Kedge ..	1	5			

40 Guns.

Anchors.	No. allowed.	Weight of each. (Cwt.)	Total Weight. (Cwt.)	Rate per Cwt. (£ s. d.)	Value. (£ s. d.)
Bower ..	4	46	184	3 1 5	565 0 8
Stream ..	1	10		2 7 3	35 8 9
Kedge ..	1	5			

38 Guns.

Anchors.	No. allowed.	Weight of each. (Cwt.)	Total Weight. (Cwt.)	Rate per Cwt. (£ s. d.)	Value. (£ s. d.)
Bower ..	4	44	176	2 17 2½	503 8 8
Stream ..	1	10		2 7 3	35 8 9
Kedge ..	1	5			

36 Guns.

Anchors.	No. allowed.	Weight of each. (Cwt.)	Total Weight. (Cwt.)	Rate per Cwt. (£ s. d.)	Value. (£ s. d.)
Bower ..	4	40	160	2 17 2½	457 13 4
Stream ..	1	10		2 7 3	35 8 9
Kedge ..	1	5			

32 Guns, large, from 910 to 972

Anchors.	No. allowed.	Weight of each. (Cwt.)	Total Weight. (Cwt.)	Rate per Cwt. (£ s. d.)	Value. (£ s. d.)
Bower ..	4	40	160	2 17 2½	457 13 4
Stream ..	1	8½		2 7 3	29 10 7
Kedge ..	1	4			

32, Smaller class, that carry 18-pounders.

Anchors.	No. allowed.	Weight of each. (Cwt.)	Total Weight. (Cwt.)	Rate per Cwt. (£ s. d.)	Value. (£ s. d.)
Bower ..	4	35	140	2 13 6½	374 15 10
Stream ..	1	8½		2 7 3	29 10 7
Kedge ..	1	4			

32 Guns, common class.

Anchors.	No. allowed.	Weight of each. (Cwt.)	Total Weight. (Cwt.)	Rate per Cwt. (£ s. d.)	Value. (£ s. d.)
Bower ..	4	32	128	2 10 6¾	323 12 0
Stream ..	1	8½		2 7 3	29 10 7
Kedge ..	1	4			

28 Guns.

Anchors.	No. allowed.	Weight of each. (Cwt.)	Total Weight. (Cwt.)	Rate per Cwt. (£ s. d.)	Value. (£ s. d.)
Bower ..	4	31	124	2 10 6½	313 9 9
Stream ..	1	8		2 7 3	28 7 0
Kedge ..	1	4			

24 Guns.

Anchors.	No. allowed.	Weight of each. (Cwt.)	Total Weight. (Cwt.)	Rate per Cwt. (£ s. d.)	Value. (£ s. d.)
Bower ..	4	29½	118	2 8 3½	284 18 5
Stream ..	1	7½		2 7 3	25 19 9
Kedge ..	1	3½			

20 Guns.

Anchors.	No. allowed.	Weight of each. (Cwt.)	Total Weight. (Cwt.)	Rate per Cwt. (£ s. d.)	Value. (£ s. d.)
Bower ..	4	25	100	2 8 3½	241 9 2
Stream ..	1	7½		2 7 3	25 19 9
Kedge ..	1	3½			

Sloops of 481 Tons.

Anchors.	No. allowed.	Weight of each. (Cwt.)	Total Weight. (Cwt.)	Rate per Cwt. (£ s. d.)	Value. (£ s. d.)
Bower ..	3	25	75	2 8 3½	181 1 10½
Stream ..	1	7½		2 7 3	25 19 9
Kedge ..	1	3½			

Sloops of 422 Tons.

Anchors.	No. allowed.	Weight of each. (Cwt.)	Total Weight. (Cwt.)	Rate per Cwt. (£ s. d.)	Value. (£ s. d.)
Bower ..	3	23	69	2 8 3½	166 12 1¾
Stream ..	1	7½		2 7 3	25 19 9
Kedge ..	1	3½			

Sloops of 361 to 422 Tons.

Anchors.	No. allowed.	Weight of each. (Cwt.)	Total Weight. (Cwt.)	Rate per Cwt. (£ s. d.)	Value. (£ s. d.)
Bower ..	3	21	63	2 8 3½	152 2 4½
Stream ..	1	7½		2 7 3	25 19 9
Kedge ..	1	3½			

Sloops 268 to 340 Tons.

Anchors.	No. allowed.	Weight of each. (Cwt.)	Total Weight. (Cwt.)	Rate per Cwt. (£ s. d.)	Value. (£ s. d.)
Bower ..	3	20	60	2 7 3	141 15 0
Stream ..	1	7½		2 7 3	25 19 9
Kedge ..	1	3½			

Brig Sloops, 370 Tons and upwards.

Anchors.	No. allowed.	Weight of each. (Cwt.)	Total Weight. (Cwt.)	Rate per Cwt. (£ s. d.)	Value. (£ s. d.)
Bower ..	3	20	60	2 7 3	141 15 0
Stream ..	1	7		2 7 3	24 16 1½
Kedge ..	1	3½			

Brig Sloops, about 365 Tons.

Anchors.	No. allowed.	Weight of each. (Cwt.)	Total Weight. (Cwt.)	Rate per Cwt. (£ s. d.)	Value. (£ s. d.)
Bower ..	3	16	48		
Stream ..	1	7		2 7 3	138 4 1⅓
Kedge ..	1	3½			

Brigs, about 313 Tons, and 282 Tons.

Anchors.	No. allowed.	Weight of each. (Cwt.)	Total Weight. (Cwt.)	Rate per Cwt. (£ s. d.)	Value. (£ s. d.)
Bower ..	3	15	45		
Stream ..	1	7		2 7 3	131 2 4½
Kedge ..	1	3½			

Brigs 250, to Gun Brigs of 187 Tons.

Anchors.	No. allowed.	Weight of each. (Cwt.)	Total Weight. (Cwt.)	Rate per Cwt. (£ s. d.)	Value. (£ s. d.)
Bower ..	3	14	42		
Stream ..	1	5		2 7 3	115 5 3
Kedge ..	1	2			

Establishment and value of anchors for ships of each class in the British Navy, 1809. (From Burney's *Marine Dictionary* of 1815)

Table of Dimensions of Anchors and Cables in Proportion to the Ship, from Hedderwick, 1830

Ship's Tonnage	Anchors with Wood Stock and Hemp Cable			Anchors with Iron Stock and Hemp Cable			Girth of Cable	Anchors for Wood Stock and Chain Cable			Anchors for Iron Stock and Chain Cable			Diameter of Chain	Weight per Fathom	Acraman's average Proof Strain	
																With Cross bars	Without Cross Bars
10	1	0	4	1	0	27	5¾	0	3	26	1	0	10	$9/16$	18	5	4
20	1	2	20	2	0	2	6⅝	1	2	11	1	3	15	$5/8$	25	6	5
30	2	0	22	2	2	15	7¼	2	0	10	2	2	1	$11/16$	28	7.5	6
40	2	3	0	3	1	6	7¾	2	2	13	3	1	5	$23/32$, or ¾	30	10	7.4
50	3	1	4	3	3	22	8⅛	3	0	14	3	3	0	¾	33		
60	3	3	8	4	2	6	8⅝	3	2	16	4	1	12	$13/16$	38	11.1	8.8
70	4	1	10	5	0	23	9	4	0	14	4	3	22	$7/8$	45	13	9.16
80	4	3	8	5	3	4	9⅜	4	2	9	5	2	0	$7/8$	45		
90	5	1	4	6	1	10	9⅝	5	0	3	6	0	3	$29/32$	48		
100	5	3	6	6	3	24	9⅞	5	2	2	6	2	3	$15/16$	52	15	11
110	6	1	4	7	2	4	10⅛	5	3	25	7	0	19	$15/16$	52		
120	6	3	2	8	0	14	10⅜	6	1	21	7	2	25	1	59	18	14
130	7	0	26	8	2	20	10⅝	6	3	14	8	1	0	1	59		
140	7	2	24	9	1	1	10⅞	7	1	9	8	3	5	$1 1/16$	64	22	
160	8	2	20	10	1	18	11⅜	8	1	0	9	3	17	$1 1/16$	64		
180	9	2	18	11	2	10	11¾	9	0	20	11	0	1	1⅛	72	26	
200	10	2	12	12	2	25	12⅛	10	0	9	12	0	11	1⅛	72		
220	11	2	5	13	3	11	12½	10	3	25	13	0	19	$1 3/16$	79	29	
240	12	1	27	14	3	27	12¾	11	3	13	14	0	27	$1 5/16$	79		
260	13	1	21	16	0	14	13⅛	12	3	2	15	1	8	1¼	88	32	
280	14	1	15	17	1	1	13⅜	13	2	14	16	1	11	1¼	88		
300	15	1	8	18	1	15	13¾	14	2	7	17	1	25	$1 5/16$	98	35	
320	16	1	0	19	2	0	14	15	1	21	18	2	3	$1 5/16$	98		
360	18	0	13	21	3	19	14½	17	0	24	20	2	17	1⅜	110	38	
400	20	0	0	24	0	0	15	19	0	0	22	3	5	$1 13/32$	112		
440	21	3	9	26	0	22	15½	20	3	0	24	3	15	$1 7/16$	115	41	
480	23	2	20	28	1	18	15⅞	22	2	0	27	0	0	1½	125	44	
500	24	2	11	29	2	2	16⅛	23	1	14	28	0	5	1½	125	44	
550	26	3	14	32	0	27	16½	25	2	4	30	2	16	$1 9/16$	134	48	
600	29	0	15	34	3	23	16⅞	27	2	20	33	0	24	$1 9/16$	134		
650	31	1	13	37	2	15	17⅜	29	3	6	35	3	1	1⅝	146	52	
700	33	2	10	40	1	6	17¾	31	3	18	38	1	5	$1 21/32$	150		
750	35	3	7	42	3	25	18⅛	34	0	3	40	3	9	$1 11/16$	158		
800	38	0	5	45	2	17	18½	36	0	16	43	1	13	$1 23/32$, or ¾	170		
900	42	1	18	50	3	16	19¼	40	1	5	48	1	11	$1 13/16$	176		
1000	46	2	20	56	0	1	19⅞	44	1	11	53	0	24	$1 27/32$	184		
1100	50	3	10				20⅜							1⅞	195		
1200	54	3	15				21							$1 15/16$	211		
1300	58	3	6				21½							2	230		

TABLE of the dimensions of Anchors, as made in his Majesty's dock-yards, from 1cwt. to 90, which is the weight of the largest Anchors used in the first rates.

Weight.	Length of the shank.		Length of the flooks.		Breadth of the palms.		Thickness of the palms.		Size of the trend.		Size of the small round.		Outer diamet. of the ring.		Thickness of the ring.	
cwt.	feet.	in.	feet.	in.	feet.	in.	feet.	in.	feet.	in.	feet.	in.	feet.	in.	feet.	in.
1	5	8	1	10	0	9	0	0¼	0	2½	0	2	0	9	0	1
2	6	6	2	2	0	11	0	0¼	0	2¼	0	2¼	0	11	0	1⅛
3	7	0	2	4	1	0	0	0⅞	0	3	0	2½	1	0	0	1¼
4	7	6	2	6	1	1	0	0⅞	0	3¼	0	2¾	1	1	0	1⅜
5	8	0	2	8	1	2	0	1	0	3½	0	3	1	2	0	1½
6	8	6	2	10	1	3	0	1	0	3¾	0	3¼	1	3	0	1⅝
7	9	0	3	0	1	4	0	1	0	4	0	3½	1	4	0	1¾
8	9	6	3	2	1	5	0	1⅛	0	4¼	0	3¾	1	5	0	1⅞
9	10	0	3	4	1	6	0	1⅛	0	4⅜	0	3⅞	1	6	0	1 15/16
10	10	4	3	5	1	7	0	1⅛	0	4½	0	4	1	7	0	2
11	0	8	3	7	1	8	0	1¼	0	4⅝	0	4⅛	1	8	0	2 1/16
12	11	0	3	8	1	8¼	0	1¼	0	4⅝	0	4⅛	1	8¼	0	2 1/16
13	11	4	3	10	1	8½	0	1¼	0	4¾	0	4¼	1	8½	0	2⅛
14	11	8	3	11	1	8¾	0	1¼	0	4⅞	0	4⅜	1	8¾	0	2 3/16
15	12	0	4	0	1	9	0	1⅜	0	5	0	4½	1	9	0	2¼
16	12	3	4	1	1	9⅛	0	1⅜	0	5⅛	0	4⅝	1	9⅛	0	2 5/16
17	12	6	4	2	1	9¼	0	1⅜	0	5¼	0	4¾	1	9¼	0	2⅜
18	12	8	4	3	1	9½	0	1⅜	0	5⅜	0	4⅞	1	9½	0	2 7/16
19	12	10	4	4	1	9⅝	0	1½	0	5½	0	5	1	9⅝	0	2½
20	13	0	4	4½	1	9¾	0	1½	0	5⅝	0	5⅛	1	9¾	0	2 9/16
21	13	2	4	5	1	9¾	0	1½	0	5⅞	0	5⅛	1	9¾	0	2 9/16
22	13	4	4	5⅜	1	10	0	1½	0	6⅛	0	5⅜	1	10	0	2 11/16
23	13	6	4	6	1	10¼	0	1½	0	6¼	0	5½	1	10¼	0	2¾
24	13	8	4	6½	1	10½	0	1½	0	6⅜	0	5⅝	1	10½	0	2 13/16
25	13	10	4	7	1	11	0	1⅝	0	6½	0	5¾	1	11	0	2⅞
26	14	0	4	8	1	11½	0	1⅝	0	6⅝	0	5⅞	1	11½	0	2 15/16
27	14	2	4	8½	1	11¾	0	1⅝	0	6⅝	0	5⅞	1	11¾	0	2 15/16
28	14	4	4	9¼	1	11¾	0	1⅝	0	6⅝	0	5⅞	1	11¾	0	2 15/16
29	14	6	4	10	2	0	0	1¾	0	6⅝	0	5⅞	2	0	0	2 15/16
30	14	7½	4	10½	2	0½	0	1¾	0	6¾	0	6	2	0½	0	3
31	14	9	4	11	2	1	0	1⅞	0	6¾	0	6	2	1	0	3
32	14	10	4	11½	2	1½	0	1⅞	0	6⅞	0	6⅛	2	1½	0	3 1/16
33	15	0	5	0	2	1¾	0	1⅞	0	7	0	6¼	2	1¾	0	3⅛
34	15	1	5	0¼	2	2	0	2	0	7¼	0	6½	2	2	0	3¼
35	15	2	5	0⅜	2	2½	0	2	0	7⅜	0	6⅝	2	2½	0	3 5/16
36	15	4	5	1¼	2	2¾	0	2	0	7½	0	6¾	2	2¾	0	3⅜
37	15	6	5	2	2	3	0	2	0	7½	0	6¾	2	3	0	3⅜
38	15	7	5	2¼	2	3½	0	2⅛	0	7⅝	0	6⅞	2	3½	0	3 7/16
39	15	9	5	3	2	3¾	0	2¼	0	7⅝	0	6⅞	2	3¾	0	3 7/16
40	15	10	5	3½	2	4	0	2⅜	0	7¾	0	7	2	4	0	3½
41	16	0	5	4	2	4¼	0	2½	0	7¾	0	7	2	4¼	0	3½
42	16	1	5	4¼	2	4½	0	2½	0	7¾	0	7	2	4½	0	3½
43	16	2	5	4½	2	5	0	2½	0	7⅞	0	7⅛	2	5	0	3 9/16
44	16	3	5	5	2	5¼	0	2½	0	7⅞	0	7⅛	2	5¼	0	3 9/16
45	16	4	5	5¼	2	5½	0	2½	0	8	0	7¼	2	5½	0	3⅝
46	16	5	5	5½	2	5¾	0	2½	0	8	0	7¼	2	5¾	0	3⅝
47	16	6	5	6	2	6	0	2½	0	8⅛	0	7⅜	2	6	0	3 11/16
48	16	7	5	6¼	2	6¼	0	2½	0	8⅛	0	7⅜	2	6¼	0	3 11/16
49	16	8	5	6½	2	6½	0	2⅝	0	8	0	7⅜	2	6½	0	3 11/16
50	16	9	5	6¾	2	7	0	2⅝	0	8¼	0	7½	2	7	0	3¾

Continuation of Table.

Weight.	Length of the shank.		Length of the flooks.		Breadth of the palms.		Thickness of palms.		Size of the trend.		Size of small round.		Outer diamet. of the ring.		Thickness of the ring.	
cwt.	feet.	in.	feet.	in.	feet.	in.	feet.	in.	feet.	in.	feet.	in.	feet.	in.	feet.	in.
51	16	10	5	7	2	7½	0	2⅝	0	8¼	0	7½	2	7½	0	3¾
52	16	11	5	7½	2	8	0	2⅝	0	8¼	0	7½	2	8	0	3¾
53	17	0	5	7¾	2	8¼	0	2⅝	0	8⅜	0	7⅝	2	8¼	0	3 13/16
54	17	1	5	8¼	2	8⅝	0	2⅝	0	8⅜	0	7⅝	2	8⅝	0	3 13/16
55	17	2	5	8½	2	9	0	2¾	0	8½	0	7¾	2	9	0	3⅞
56	17	3	5	9	2	9¼	0	2¾	0	8½	0	7¾	2	9¼	0	3⅞
57	17	4	5	9½	2	9½	0	2¾	0	8½	0	7¾	2	9½	0	3⅞
58	17	5	5	9¾	2	10	0	2¾	0	8¾	0	7⅞	2	10	0	3 15/16
59	17	6	5	10	2	10¼	0	2¾	0	8⅝	0	7⅞	2	10¼	0	3 15/16
60	17	7	5	10¼	2	10½	0	2⅞	0	8¾	0	7⅞	2	10½	0	3 15/16
61	17	8	5	10½	2	11	0	3	0	8¾	0	8	2	11	0	4
62	17	9	5	11	2	11½	0	3	0	8¾	0	8	2	11½	0	4
63	17	10	5	11¼	2	11¾	0	3	0	8⅞	0	8	2	11¾	0	4
64	17	11	5	11¾	3	0	0	3	0	8⅞	0	8	3	0	0	4
65	18	0	6	0	3	0	0	3⅛	0	9	0	8	3	0	0	4
66	18	1	6	0¼	3	0	0	3⅛	0	9	0	8	3	0	0	4
67	18	2	6	0½	3	1	0	3⅛	0	9	0	8	3	1	0	4
68	18	3	6	1	3	1	0	3⅛	0	9⅛	0	8	3	1	0	4
69	18	3½	6	1⅛	3	1	0	3⅛	0	9⅛	0	8	3	1	0	4
70	18	4	6	1¼	3	1	0	3¼	0	9¼	0	8⅛	3	1	0	4 1/16
71	18	5	6	1½	3	1½	0	3¼	0	9¼	0	8⅛	3	1½	0	4 1/16
72	18	6	6	2	3	1½	0	3¼	0	9¼	0	8⅛	3	1½	0	4 1/16
73	18	8	6	2½	3	1½	0	3¼	0	9⅜	0	8⅛	3	1½	0	4 1/16
74	18	9½	6	3	3	1½	0	3⅜	0	9⅜	0	8⅛	3	1½	0	4 1/16
75	18	11	6	3½	3	1½	0	3⅜	0	9⅜	0	8⅛	3	1½	0	4 1/16
76	19	0⅜	6	4⅛	3	2	0	3⅜	0	9⅜	0	8⅛	3	2	0	4 1/16
77	19	1¾	6	4⅝	3	2	0	3½	0	9½	0	8 3/16	3	2	0	4⅛
78	19	3⅜	6	5	3	2	0	3½	0	9¼	0	8 3/16	3	2	0	4⅛
79	19	4½	6	5½	3	2	0	3½	0	9¾	0	8¼	3	2	0	4⅛
80	19	6	6	6	3	2	0	3½	0	9¾	0	8¼	3	2	0	4⅛
81	19	8	6	6⅝	3	2½	0	3⅝	0	10	0	8¼	3	2½	0	4⅛
82	19	8	6	6⅝	3	2½	0	3⅝	0	10	0	8¼	3	2½	0	4⅛
83	19	8	6	6⅝	3	2¾	0	3⅝	0	10	0	8⅜	3	3½	0	4¼
84	19	9	6	7	3	3	0	3⅝	0	10⅛	0	8⅜	3	3	0	4¼
85	19	9	6	7	3	3¼	0	3⅝	0	10⅛	0	8⅜	3	3¼	0	4¼
86	19	9	6	7	3	3⅜	0	3⅝	0	10⅛	0	8⅜	3	3⅜	0	4¼
87	19	10	6	7¼	3	3⅜	0	3¾	0	10⅛	0	8½	3	3⅜	0	4⅜
88	19	10	6	7¼	3	3½	0	3¾	0	10¼	0	8½	3	3½	0	4⅜
89	19	10	6	7¼	3	3½	0	3¾	0	10¼	0	8½	3	3½	0	4⅜
90	19	11	6	7⅝	3	3⅝	0	3¾	0	10¼	0	8½	3	3⅝	0	4⅜

Table of the dimensions of anchors, as made in his Majesty's dockyards, from 1 cwt to 90 cwt, which is the largest anchors used in First Rates, 1809. (From Burney's *Marine Dictionary* of 1815)

8 | The construction of anchors

A 25 hundredweight sheet or bower anchor for a 20-gun ship, surrounded by vignettes of the principal pieces of equipment used in the forging of anchors. Plate from David Steel's Naval Architecture, *1793. (National Maritime Museum C6996/a)*

Anchors were largely forged in the Naval Dockyards, and made up of pieces of iron, often scrap iron, welded together. These were heated to a white heat, then beaten into a solid mass, initially by manual sledge hammers, later by mechanical drop hammers. Separate pieces were then shaped into the shank of

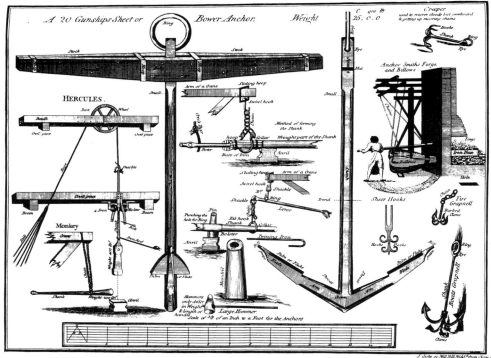

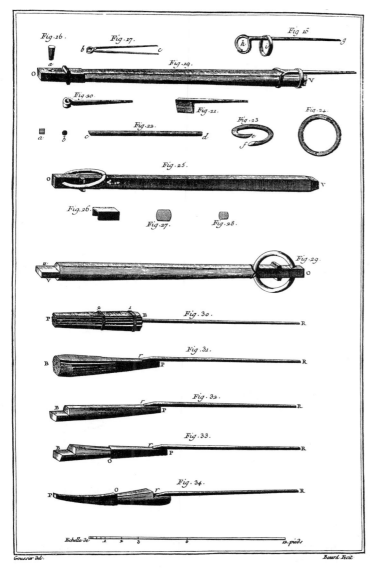

Constituent parts of an anchor before forging; the lever-like extensions provide a method of handling the parts during forging, and are cut off when required. (From Diderot's *Encylopédie*, Vol VII Marine, Forges des Ancres, 1763: Plate VIII)

the anchor. The flukes were prepared in the same way, and welded to the arms before the latter were married to the shank. The large iron anchor ring having been forged and shaped would be rove through the head of the shank and welded into it. Bands to secure the two parts of the wooden stock would be prepared on a smaller forge.

Welding, in the original meaning of the term, as employed

Forging an anchor: squaring the crown of the shank, with the aid of a water-driven trip hammer. Where there was an insufficient head of water, a team of men hauling on a rope could work either a drop hammer or a manual version of the trip hammer. (From Diderot's *Encylopédie*, Vol VII Marine, Forges des Ancres, 1763: Plate VII)

by smiths, signifies the joining of heated metal by pressure applied. The areas of the joints were called 'scarphs', and smiths naturally had their own way of scarphing the pieces – that is, welding them together in a form to produce the shape and length required without the joins being apparent. Scarphing was also used extensively by shipwrights working with timber

The Old Admiralty pattern anchor survived to the early years of the nineteenth century, despite a tendency for the straight arms to break off at the crown when over-stressed. The hammering process during welding was incapable of expelling all the air and bubbles formed at the join between the arm and the shank produced a particular area of weakness. During the vast expansion in manufacturing brought about by the Napoleonic Wars, the Navy Board became increasingly concerned about failures, and in the three years from 1809 over 300 anchors were returned to the Naval Dockyards for repair. The situation was saved by a quantum leap in the quality of iron and the consequent revolution in anchor manufacture, as detailed in the following section.

Henry Cort's iron

In March 1787 'A Brief Statement of Facts relative to the New Method of making Bar Iron discovered and brought to perfection by Mr Henry Cort of Gosport' described the severe tests successfully passed by his iron, which was 'afterwards distributed to all the Royal Dockyards'.

> Mr Cort's process of refining Iron from the pig, or cast state, in a reverberatory furnace, heated by common coal, or any other fuel, has the effect of separating from the metallic particles, certain impurities which are not discharged in the common methods of rendering Iron malleable, and therefore a manifest difference of quality is occasioned in favour of the furnace Iron: which quality is further improved by the mode, also invented by Mr Cort, and used in manufacturing the Iron, when malleable, into bars, and even into bolts and many uses, by rolling it in a welding heat, through rollers with grooves accurately formed, instead of working it under hammers. This Iron has a peculiar appearance in its grain, but it is

Forging an anchor: welding the fluke to the arm. Note the extension piece being used to hold the arm in place. (From Diderot's *Encylopédie*, Vol VII Marine, Forges des Ancres, 1763: Plate IX)

nevertheless so effectually disentangled from impure scoria, and the texture of it is so uniformly perfect, that it may be pronounced superior, on the whole, for body, strength and toughness, even to the best sort of Swedish Orground's Iron. Mr Cort manufactured about thirty tons of this Iron, under the inspection of two master smiths belonging to the King's dockyards, from old ship-ballast delivered to him out of the dockyard at Portsmouth for that purpose. The Bar Iron so made by Mr Cort was afterwards distributed to all the Royal Dockyards, and being there wrought into anchors, and other naval implements, underwent a series of experiments, against the like instruments wrought from the best Orground's Iron, whereby its qualities were put to the severest test.

A long list follows of the 'comparable experiments' undergone by Swedish Orground's iron and by Cort's iron taking place at Portsmouth, Deptford, Woolwich, Sheerness, Chatham and Plymouth, in each case giving careful details of the trials in matched printed columns and with results of the tests applied. In Plymouth's case, the Master Smith of this yard expressed his opinion that 'Mr Cort's Iron, used in the articles which were the subjects of the above experiments, is equal to any he ever made use of.'

A variety of authorities were equally satisfied with the merits of Henry Cort's iron. In 'General Remarks' on the tests, an anonymous writer quoted the annual tonnage of iron imported from Sweden and Russia plus that made in England–about 100,000 tons–and pointed out that of all this only Orground's 20,000 tons was esteemed 'of sufficient strength . . . for anchor etc, . . . and other iron work belonging to the building, rigging and navigation of ships, upon the perfect goodness of which the lives and safety of so many of His Majesty's useful subjects, the seamen of Great Britain depend'.

This writer went on to remark that although the quantity of bar iron made in England and Scotland, about 30,000 tons, might not satisfy the demand at present, this was partly due to the inferior quality of the product. 'Many more blast furnaces might be worked, if they were encouraged by a demand for pig iron, equal to what Mr Cort's discovery must occasion when it is brought into general use. The raw materials are in a manner inexhaustible.' He concluded by observing:

Forging an anchor: welding an arm to the shank. For an effective weld, both parts need to be heated simultaneously, so there are two forges, with the cranes arranged to swing shank and arm from fire to anvil with the least delay. (From Diderot's *Encylopédie*, Vol VII Marine, Forges des Ancres, 1763: Plate X)

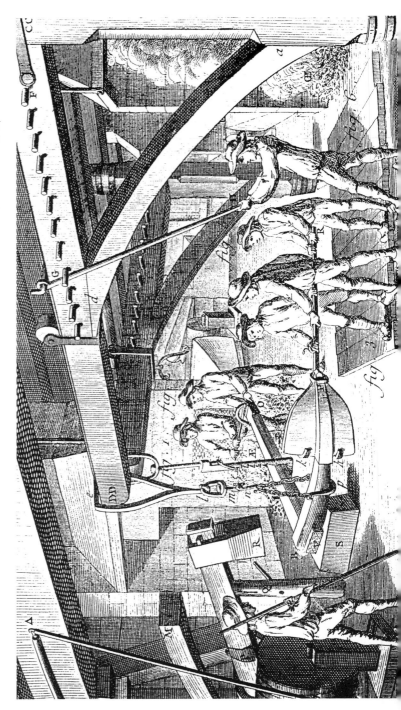

On the whole, not withstanding the expenses unavoidably incidental to such a discovery in its infant state, this Iron can be afforded at a cheaper price to be paid at home, than has been necessarily paid to foreigners for an article so very important to government and nation, as the Swedish Orground's Iron, on which the preservation of His Majesty's fleet has hitherto depended, but to which the Iron manufactured according to this discovery has been proved equal for use in all respects and superior in many. Among these it cannot escape observation that in all five different trials upon large anchors weighing from 34 to 59cwt, those made of the [Cort's] furnace refined Iron had a manifest superiority over those of Orground's Iron.

In happy contrast to the present-day valuation of heavy industry, the significance of this development was fully appreciated at the time. The following extract from Lord Sheffield's *Observations on the Commerce of the American States*, written in the years following American independence, confirms this.

If Mr Cort's very ingenious and meritorious improvements in the art of making and working Iron, and his invention of making bar Iron from pig Iron . . . and the great improvements on the steam engines by Messrs. Watt and Bolton of Birmingham, and Lord Dundonald's discovery of making coke for the furnace, at half the present expense, should all succeed, as there is reason to think they will, the expense may be reduced so greatly, that British Iron may be afforded as cheap as foreign even if the latter should be allowed to enter duty free, perhaps cheaper, and of as improved a quality and in quantity equal to the demand. It is not asserting too much to say that event would be more advantageous to Britain than Thirteen Colonies. It would give the complete command of the Iron trade to this country, with its vast advantages to navigation. Our knowledge in the Iron trade seems hitherto to have been in its infancy.

All these extracts quoted are taken, by courtesy of Edinburgh University Library, from the Joseph Black papers in their care. In May 1786 Dr Joseph Black was Professor of Chemistry at Edinburgh, and saw experiments there which proved Mr Cort's

Forging an anchor: welding the second arm to the shank. Both sides of the crown need to be hammered, so there is an arrangement to turn the whole assembly over. (From Diderot's *Encylopédie*, Vol VII Marine, Forges des Ancres, 1763: Plate XI)

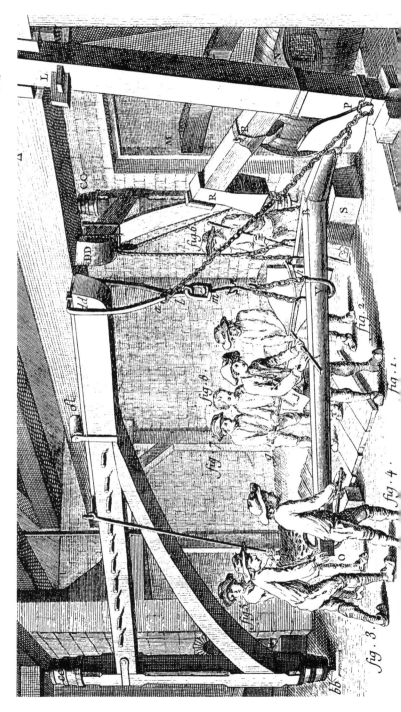

Iron 'to be possessed of very great strength and toughness'. The only point on which he was undecided was 'whether it could be afforded sufficiently cheap'. Messrs Folliot, Scott and Company, of the Rotherhithe Iron Works, had no such doubts. In March 1787 they wrote to Messrs Cort and Jellicoe as follows:

> Gentlemen,
> We have the pleasure to inform you that we are now fully able to make Iron upon the principles laid down in your specification, and in as great perfection as we flattered ourselves we could attain to. We shall be happy to show any friends of yours such proofs as we doubt not will be perfectly satisfactory to demonstrate the superior excellence both of the process and the Iron made under your licence.
>
> We need not inform you, that your Patent Rollers and the Hammer are worked by Messrs. Boulton and Watts Steam Engine, but we must observe, that it has all the effects we wish or could have expected.
> We are very sincerely, Gentlemen, Your most obedient Servants
> Folliot, Scott & Company

If the length of this account of Henry Cort's new process of refining iron seems excessive, it is hoped that the great importance of his 'discovery' will excuse it. The above quotations suggest its tremendous impact and results. Returning specifically to anchors, the new iron technology provided opportunities for improved manufacture, and in retrospect it seems that an advance in their design was also inevitable, as later chapters will show.

Forging an anchor: finishing the crown, by the use of a cold chisel to remove surface imperfections. (From Diderot's *Encylopédie*, Vol VII Marine, Forges des Ancres, 1763: Plate XII)

Anchor designers of the nineteenth century | 9

Richard Pering

The Board of Admiralty having used the Old Admiralty Longshank anchor for most of the 1700s, even its most diehard members must have accepted the possibility of improved types. At the height of the Napoleonic Wars there was something of a crisis with the traditional model. Of the large numbers returned to English Naval Dockyards for repairs, records for three years from late 1809 listed 350 repaired and 150 still outstanding. This kind of pressure, along with the development of Henry Cort's iron and, later, of James Nasmyth's steam hammer opened the way for the new designers.

Richard Pering, born in 1765 or 1770, was apprenticed at the age of twelve to John Henshaw, shipwright of Dartmouth, for £87 from March 1782, according to family records. Five years later he was a shipwright himself, and by 1809 Clerk of the Cheque at Plymouth Dockyard. He was offering proposals for new types of anchors from 1800 onwards. They must have had some merit for in 1801 a reply from the Navy Office suggested that 'the adoption of these at present would occasion so many applications for a change of anchors of the Fleet that it were better deferred till peace afforded better opportunity for trials.' Not surprisingly, although the Navy Board offered 'every support and assistance', wartime progress was slow. A trial anchor was made by Brunton & Co, and there followed a long correspondence with the Board. One of Pering's anchors broke, possibly because the arms, like the Old Admiralty Longshank's, were straight. Pering's attention was then focussed particularly on this point of weakness and its possible improvement.

He also produced a plan for a pit lined with bricks for use in turning the anchor over in the welding process, and suggested that the completed anchor should be annealed, *ie* heated and slowly cooled at an even rate. Notably, he criticised the practice of polishing the anchor with hammer blows to conceal hidden defects. His important innovation was that flat instead of round bars should be welded together in an arrangement which rounded the junction of arms to shank, and moved the scarph (the point of junction of the prepared iron bars, see Chapter 8) away from the point of greatest stress. More powerful mechan-

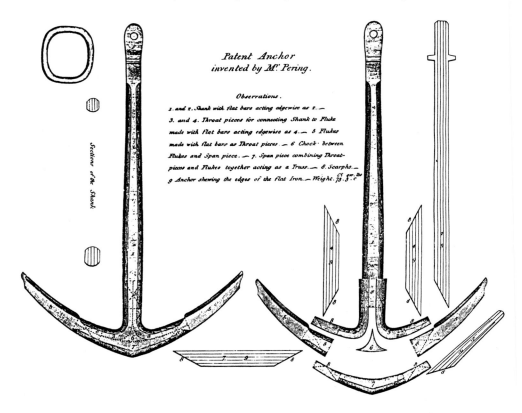

The method of anchor construction patented by Richard Pering in July 1813. The figures on the drawing are keyed as follows: 1 and 2. Shank with flat bars acting edgewise as 2. - 3 and 4. Throat pieces for connecting Shank to Fluke made with flat bars acting edgewise at 4. - 5. Flukes made with flat bars as Throat pieces. - 6. Chock between Flukes and Span piece. - 7. Span piece combining Throat-pieces and Flukes together acting as a Truss. - 8. Scarphs. - 9. Anchor shewing the edges of the flat Iron. - Weight 73cwt. 3qrs. 0lbs. (From Pering's Treatise on the Anchor, 1819)

Weight and Length of Anchors supplied to the different Classes of Ships, from Fincham, 1825

Class of ship	Guns / Tons	Weight of Anchors supplied — No	cwt	qr	Whole Length Pering — ft	in	Common — ft	in	Ring to Bill Pering — ft	in	Common — ft	in	Extreme End to Bill Pering — ft	in	Common — ft	in	Of Stream — No	cwt	qr	Of Kedge — No	cwt	qr
Three-deck ships	**Guns** 120	4	95	0	18	7¾	19	2¾	14	10	15	5	15	5	16	0	1	21	0	1	5	0
																				1	10	2
	110	4	90	0	18	4¾	19	0¼	14	7	15	2	15	2	15	9	1	21	0	1	5	0
																				1	10	2
	104	4	84	0	18	1½	18	8½	14	4	14	11	14	11	15	6	1	21	0	1	5	0
																				1	10	2
	98	4	76	0	17	7½	18	2	13	11	14	6	13	5	15	1	1	18	0	1	4	2
																				1	9	0
Two-deck ships	86	4	81	0	17	11¾	18	6¼	14	2	14	10	14	8	15	4	1	18	0	1	4	2
																				1	9	0
	84	4	81	0	17	11¾	18	6¼	14	2	14	10	14	8	15	4	1	18	0	1	4	2
																				1	9	0
	82	4	76	0	17	7½	18	2	13	11	14	6	14	5	15	1	1	18	0	1	4	2
																				1	9	0
	80	4	76	0	17	7½	18	2	13	11	14	6	14	5	15	1	1	18	0	1	4	2
																				1	9	0
	78	4	76	0	17	7½	18	2	13	11	14	6	14	5	15	1	1	17	0	1	4	2
																				1	8	2
	76	4	76	0	17	7½	18	2	13	11	14	6	14	5	15	1	1	17	0	1	4	2
																				1	8	2
	74	4	76	0	17	7½	18	2	13	11	14	6	14	5	15	1	1	17	0	1	4	2
																				1	8	2
	58	4	49	0	15	6½	16	0	12	4	12	9	12	10	13	3	1	11	0	1	5	2
Built as frigates	60	4	57	0	16	1	16	7	12	9	13	3	13	3	13	8	1	15	0	1	7	2
	50	4	48	0	15	5½	15	11	12	3	12	8	12	8	13	2	1	12	0	1	5	0
	48	4	48	0	15	5½	15	11	12	3	12	8	12	8	13	2	1	12	0	1	5	0
	46	4	46	0	15	3½	15	9	12	1	12	7	12	6	13	0	1	10	0	1	5	0
	44	4	42	0	14	11½	15	5	11	10	12	4	12	3	12	9	1	10	0	1	5	0
	42	4	42	0	14	11½	15	5	11	10	12	4	12	3	12	9	1	10	0	1	5	0
	34	3	29	2	13	11	14	4	11	4	11	5	11	6	11	10	1	8	0	1	3	2
	32	3	29	2	13	11	14	4	11	4	11	5	11	6	11	10	1	8	0	1	3	2
	28	3	25	0	13	2½	13	7	10	5	10	10	10	9	11	3	1	7	0	1	3	2
	Tons 26	3	23	0	12	10½	13	3	10	2	10	7	10	6	11	11	1	7	0	1	3	2
Flush-deck Vessels	455 20	3	25	0	13	2½	13	7	10	5	10	10	10	9	11	3	1	7	0	1	3	2
	460 18	2	22	0	12	8½	13	1	10	1	10	6	10	5	10	10	1	7	0	1	3	2
		1	25	0	13	2½	13	7	10	5	10	10	10	9	11	3						
	400 18	2	20	0	12	6	12	10	9	10	10	3	10	2	10	7	1	7	0	1	3	2
		1	21	0	12	6½	12	11	9	11	10	4	10	3	10	8	1					
	382 18	3	20	0	12	6	12	10	9	10	10	3	10	2	10	7	1	7	0	1	3	2
	255 16	3	20	0	12	6	12	10	9	10	10	3	10	2	10	7	1	7	0	1	3	2
	235 10	3	17	0	11	10	12	2	9	4	9	9	10	7	10	0	1	6	0	1	3	0
Cutters	160 10	3	10	2	9	8¼	9	11½	7	8	7	11	7	11	8	2						

NOTE. These lengths are taken from the establishments; but it will be found that anchors frequently vary considerably from them, it would therefore be most correct, when circumstances will allow in determining the place of the cathead, to stow the anchors properly in relation to the dead-eyes, and fixing the bill board and anchor linings, to take the dimensions from the anchors that are appropriate to the ship.

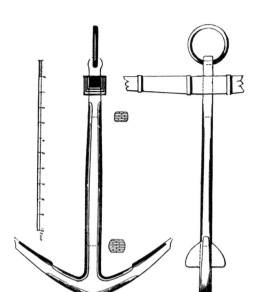
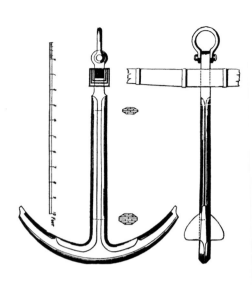

Pering's original pattern (left) and Improved Anchors. (From George Cotsell's A Treatise on Ships' Anchors, *1856)*

ical hammers used in welding assisted by expelling air bubbles from the join, and, most of all, strength was improved by the availability of Henry Cort's new iron. Curved arms meant their sectional form was oval, and the sides were flattened, not round. The shanks were noticeably shorter than those of the Old Admiralty Longshank, and the flukes likewise were smaller.

Finally, in 1813 an anchor was manufactured to his plan, tested by the Board in 1815, and thereafter approved and adopted for use in the Royal Navy. Even this pattern occasionally failed, and Pering's Improved Anchor was produced in

Model of Pering's Improved Anchor, 1829. (National Maritime Museum C8837/21a)

1835 in response. For a considerable number of years his innovations made him the foremost designer in England. The notably more curved arms of his Improved Anchor of 1835 foreshadowed the anchor approved by Admiral Sir William Parker's Board of 1841.

Not only did Richard Pering design anchors, but he also published three books on shipbuilding, most importantly in 1819 his *Treatise on the Anchor*. This was dedicated to Admirals and other 'Naval persons' in proper and graceful form. His conclusion was not so happy, and also strangely familiar.

> Had I foreseen the fatigue and inconvenience to which I have been subjected in this undertaking I am uncertain if my fortitude would have supported me through it. I have been led on, not by insensible degrees to the present moment for the space of 19 years, but more by the opposition experienced.

His obituary in *The Gentleman's Magazine* in 1838 reported that he had been an active Magistrate in Devon, as well as the designer of his Improved Anchor, which is 'used by every ship in His Majesty's Navy, and has been the means of saving thousands of lives and property to an immense extent'.

Model of an early Porter Anchor with iron stock. (National Maritime Museum C8818)

Porter and John Trotman

Other designers of the period experienced similar difficulties. John Trotman found the Higher Authority referred to earlier too much for him. The 'Phantom Lords of Naval Misrule', a phrase he used in one of his many aggressive pamphlets, defeated his attempts to have his anchor adopted throughout the British Navy, and to prolong his Patent, due to expire in April 1886.

This anchor was first designed by William Porter in 1838, possibly following a similar pattern patented by William Henry Piper

Engraving of the Trotman Improved Porter, a large 95 hundredweight model with a wooden stock. (From contemporary publicity material)

in 1822. His intention was to offer good holding qualities combined with lighter weight, an attraction to the merchant service, which was always short of manpower. It was constructed in two parts, the crown and arms being one, and the shank ending in a fork the other. The crown and arms were held in the fork by a bolt, which allowed them to swivel so that when one arm was dug into the sea bed the other pressed hard on the shank. 'Horns' on the outside of the arms ensured that the lower opened, giving a positive grip. A fishbuckle was fitted to assist in stowing the anchor. The wooden stock of earlier models was later replaced by iron.

John Trotman's final improvement of this, following Honiball's work on it in 1846, was to turn the horns into broad, flat spade-like protrusions; it was patented in 1852. That year a committee of six naval officers and six shipowners was appointed by the Board of Admiralty to determine the best of eight anchors competing. The committee found that the Trotman anchor was best and, in performance, 28 per cent better than the Admiralty pattern.

Palm detail of the Trotman Anchor. (From George Cotsell's A Treatise on Ships' Anchors, 1856)

The *Illustrated London News* of 17 July 1852 reported 'The Trial of Anchors of All Nations at the Royal Dockyard, Sheerness 1852'.

Several very important experiments have recently been made to test the relative merits of the various anchors now in use. The investigations have been of so interesting a character that our Artist represented a scene of the trial . . . A committee of five – one short of the original six – representing the shipowners of Great Britain spent the night at Smithson's Royal Hotel, and met at 9 am next day the Admiralty's chosen representatives at the Dockyard. These were the Commanding Officers of HMS *Waterloo*, 120 guns, *London*, 90 guns and *Monarch*, 84 guns, her Commanding Officer being also the Captain Super-intendent of the Dockyard. This committee was completed by the Master Attendant of the Dockyard, the Master of *Waterloo* and Mr F J Fegan, RN as Secretary. Captain the Hon Montagu Stopford, Commanding Officer of *Waterloo*, was chosen as Chairman.

This trial was on part of the Parade Ground, which was 'spe-cially prepared to resemble the bed of the river or an anchorage ground'. As it was 250 feet long by 30 feet wide; those digging it and clearing it of 'stones and rubbish, then filling it in again with soil of equal properties throughout' must have found their enthusiasm diminishing rapidly, specially as 'two fire-engine hoses were abundantly played into the trench until the ground was filled in'.

The newspaper gave a detailed analysis of the results, and a second series of experiments was to commence on the beach off Garrison Point, 'when the anchors will be placed in two fath-oms of water and hove up the beach'. The owners of the anchors, however, expressed themselves perfectly satisfied – as, it is hoped, did the mob of wives, children and dogs who appeared to have accompanied them.

> Judging by the results attained by the above experiments it would appear that Trotman's Improved Porter's anchor pos-sesses fully 25 per cent more holding properties on dry land than any other with which it has been tried. Mr Trotman feels that similar results will attend the subsequent trials on the beach and afloat.

His confidence was well founded. They did.

Final Results of the Anchor Trials of 1852

The Committee of 1852 listed the anchors tried in the follow-ing order:

The Illustrated London News *depiction of the 1852 trials and the anchor designs tested.*

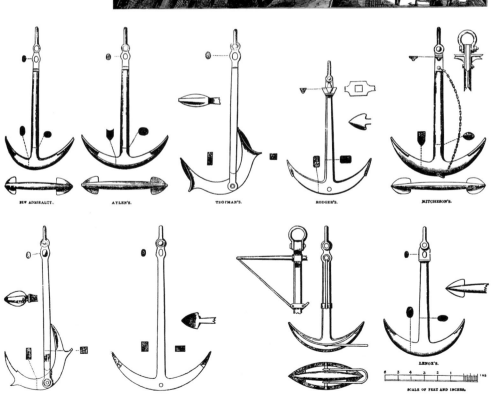

BEW ADMIRALTY.　　AYLEN'S.　　TROTMAN'S.　　RODGER'S.　　MITCHESON'S.

HONIBAL'S.　　RODGER'S.　　ISAACE'S.　　LENOX'S.

SCALE OF FEET AND INCHES.

Percentage superior to the Admiralty Anchor accepted as standard

Trotman's	28
Rodger's	26
Mitcheson's	20
Lenox's	13
Honiball's	9
Aylen's	9

Percentage inferior to the Admiralty Anchor

Isaac's	27

Encouraged by these results Trotman's hopes must have risen high, but only to be dashed. He appears a man obsessed, whose whole life was devoted to producing his anchor, and shattered when he failed to persuade the Admiralty to adopt it. At his

A large Trotman of about 38 hundredweight discovered in Canada. (National Defence Photo, by RCN)

own expense during the years 1872-1889 he published pamphlets addressed to Members of Parliament and the public, violently criticising naval expenditure and Admiralty administration. In March 1866 he petitioned Queen Victoria for his claims, pointing out that the royal yacht *Victoria and Albert* had been provided with his anchors since 1854. Also that he had sunk 'upwards of forty thousand pounds in perfecting the anchor'. He even quoted in one pamphlet a list of the First Lords of the Admiralty as including from 1833 to 1870 two dukes, three earls, one viscount, four knights and two rt. honourables – all by implication aristocratic amateurs.

A more credible cause of failure may have been that his anchor, lighter in weight than the usual Admiralty pattern but more difficult to cat and fish, was more acceptable in the merchant marine than in the Royal Navy, which had larger crews

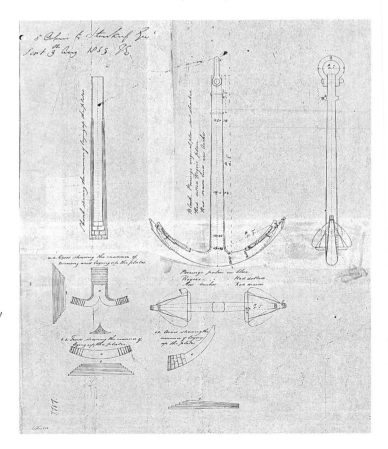

An official Admiralty draught comparing Pering's and Rodger's patterns with the 'New Anchor'. Dated 9 August 1839, it strongly suggests the provenance of the new standard Admiralty anchor of 1840-41 approved by Admiral Parker's Board. (National Maritime Museum DR7717)

An Admiralty 1841 pattern anchor with a later iron stock. (National Defence Photo, by RCN)

available for anchor handling. One success at least may have made up for his disappointments: the largest Trotman anchor ever manufactured was supplied to Isambard Kingdom Brunel's *Great Eastern* of 1858, the biggest ship in the world for a generation. She had eight anchors, six of which were Trotman's.

The Board of Admiralty anchor

The anchor officially preferred could claim weight over the technical superiority of Trotman's design. It was that developed under the aegis of Admiral Sir William Parker in 1840-41, becoming a logical evolution of Pering's Improved Anchor design. Generally considered the final development of

Key	Anchor Size
A	6'-11 1/2"
B	6 1/4"
C	5 1/16"
D	5 1/8"
E	3 5/8"
F	7 1/2" Diam.
G	7 1/2"
J	4" Diam.
K	2'-5 1/2"
L	6"
M	1'-0"
N	1 1/8"
O	5"
P	1'-1 1/2"
Q	7/8"
R	2'-11 3/8"
T	5 1/8"
Z	6"
a	10 1/2"
b	4 1/8"
c	6" Diam.
d	3 1/16" Diam.
e	3" Diam.
f	3 5/8"
n	2 3/4"
Key	**Stock Size**
H	7'-8 1/2"
I	3 1/4" Dia.
S	6"
U	5"
V	1 1/2"
W	5 1/2" Diam.
X	4 5/8" Diam.
i	2 1/2" Diam.
Key	**Forelock Size**
s	1 3/8"
k	7 1/8"
p	5/8" Dia.
h	5/8"
m	3/8" Dia.

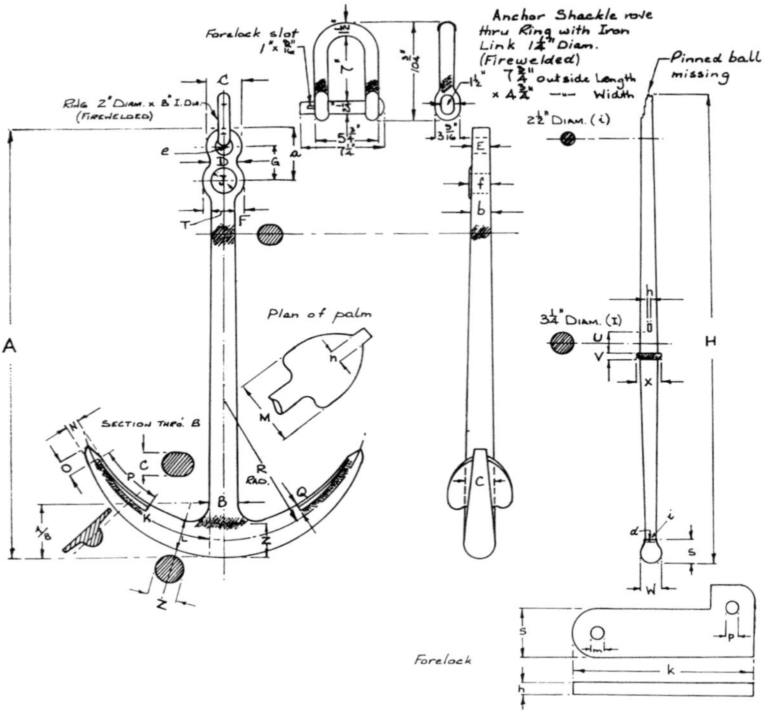

Above: *Drawing of an Admiralty 1841 pattern anchor recovered from what is believed to be the wreck of the storeship* Buffalo *lost in Mercury Bay, New Zealand, 28 July 1841.* (Royal New Zealand Navy)

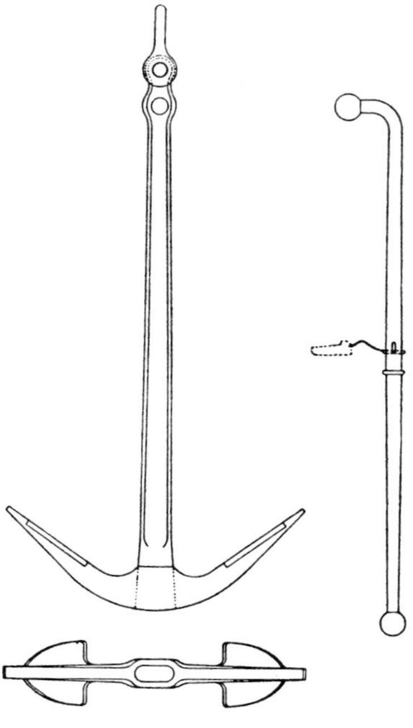

Right: *An example of the modern survival of the basic 'Admiralty' pattern, the 'Fishing Anchor' manufactured by the Baldt Anchor Co of Chester, Pennsylvania, and sanctioned by Lloyd's on 8 January 1920.* (Lloyd's Register of Shipping)

the fixed-arm anchor, it appeared in all sizes. While the proportions were very roughly the same as the old Admiralty Longshank, the arms had a graceful curve, and the iron forming them and the shank was elliptical in cross section, which eased the chafing of ropes. At first it had a wooden stock, which persisted in large bower anchors, but this was finally replaced by iron. In this form it is still widely used, specially by the smaller fishing craft without hawse pipes

Lieutenant William Rodger, RN

Of the nineteenth century's anchor designers the undaunted William Rodger, Lieutenant RN, must have knocked most frequently on the Admiralty's door. Presumably a happier man than poor Trotman but equally determined, he advanced from one design to another throughout a long naval career. Entering the Navy as a midshipman in 1808, he became Acting Master in 1811, having assisted at the capture of Guadeloupe in 1810. He

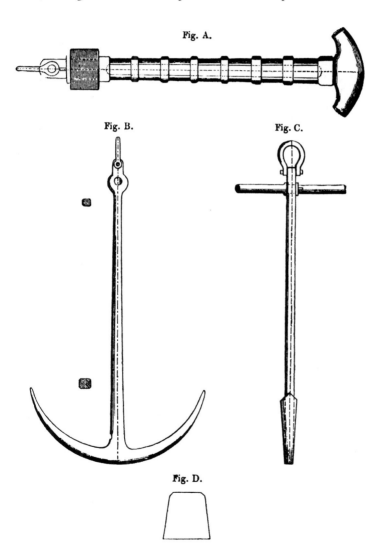

Two of Rodger's early innovations, the hollow stock and the Patent Pickaxe Anchor. (From George Cotsell's A Treatise on Ships' Anchors, *1856)*

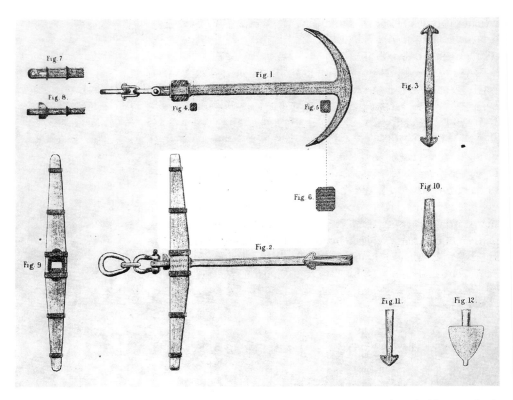

Rodger's Patent Small-Palmed Anchor. (From a contemporary advertising leaflet)

was commissioned in 1815, then was placed on half pay, which freed him to develop the inventions that made his name.

He first received from the Society for the Encouragement of Arts a Silver Medal for his plug for raising empty casks, and a year later a Gold Medal for his liferaft. Ten years after this award, he was presented with a Gold Medal for a siphon for watering ships and a Silver Medal for his 'makeshift' anchor. This last was not his first attempt at anchor design: in 1821 he designed an anchor with a hollow shank, filled with wood held in place by hoops driven over the shank, the intention being to strengthen it while reducing weight. Not surprisingly, it was unsuccessful.

Next was the Pickaxe anchor without palms (*ie* flukes) which he produced between 1830 and 1831. It resembled exactly the iron skeleton of the anchor sheathed in wood which was discovered during the draining of Lake Nemi in 1930, even to the detachable iron stock, and believed to have been forged about 1800 years earlier. The holding power of his Pickaxe Anchor

was not very great and it is tempting to wonder if its early prototype, devoid of its wooden sheath, would have had the same
difficulties in open waters.

However, in 1832-33 he produced his Patent Small-Palmed
Anchor, which was so successful that testimonials to this were
being offered as late as 1858, the patent having been sealed in
1833. Distinguished by their heart shape, the palms were
slightly increased in size in later models. This anchor, like
those preferred until the mid-nineteenth century for large
bower anchors, had a wooden stock. His design for this appears
to be almost the only weakness in his thinking. It was made in
one piece, which had to be fitted over the square end of the
shank after removing the anchor shackle, unlike the Admiralty
pattern in two halves joined by iron bands. Like the latter it had
an iron collar piece round the hole provided for the shank, but
a further disadvantage was that the slack could not be taken up
by driving the bands further on.

Writing in 1852 the then Commander Rodger indicated fur-

*A Canadian example of
a Rodger's Patent
Small-Palmed Anchor.
(National Defence
Photo, by RCN)*

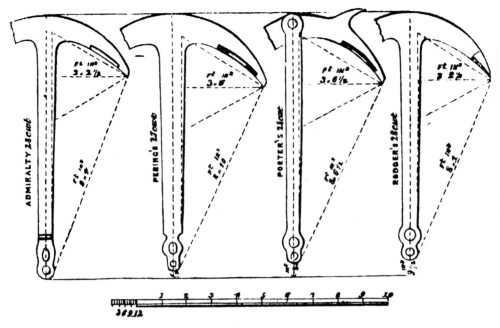

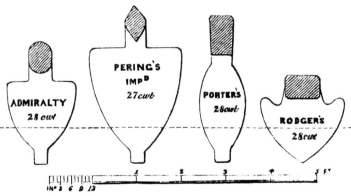

A comparison of palm sizes between standard Admiralty, Pering's, Porter's and Rodger's anchors of about 28 hundredweight. (From George Cotsell's A Treatise on Ships' Anchors, 1856)

ther improvements to his Small-Palmed Anchor. One was that the arms were to be formed on the principle of a wedge, *ie* in section they were thinner on the inside of the curve of the arm than on the outside. Unlike the Admiralty pattern the flat face of the fluke was on the outside of the arm. Of anchor palms he commented: 'From 1806 there was no alteration in the size of anchor palms; not till 1841 was the size reduced in the Royal Dockyards. At this period my first Small-Palmed anchor had been in use upwards of six years.'

His pamphlet *Explanatory Observations* dealt with the improved power of resistance of the small palm as compared with the ordinary large palm of the same weight.

> The large palm disturbs the ground in front of it, tending to rise out of the ground, then cannot be depended to take hold of it, necessitating another anchor let go. The small palm passes freely under it and penetrates deeper. Its wedge-shaped arms avoid disturbing the ground in front which closes and reunites behind it.

His only successful anchor without palms was his Patent Kedge, its arms being 3¾ inches wide at its broadest, and held well according to a much later authority, the Captain Superintendent of the Pacific Steam Navigation Company's Steam Vessels.

In 1854 Captain Rodger, as he then was, patented his Moveable Iron Stock, the wooden stock being now replaced by iron. This was a special design, constructed with the intention that the stock itself as well as the anchor should grip fast into the sea bed. His *Explanatory Observations* continue on this new iron stock:

> Its cross sections are somewhat of triangular shape, and therefore the end parts resemble a prism, with one of its angles rounded and having its front thicker than its back part, which form gives it a tendency to sink into the ground when the anchor is dragged. The stock generally rests upon its front edge; its lower side does not come wholly into contact with the ground until the crown of the anchor is buried to a considerable depth below the surface; the Improved Iron Stock sinks two to three feet below the surface. The holes in the ends of the stock are for the purpose of saving iron, where it would actually be prejudicial in some degree to the holding of the anchor. They lessen the obstruction to the sinking of the stock after the anchor is 'canted'.
>
> This stock may be shipped or unshipped in a few minutes being half as heavy as iron stocks in common use, and there-fore superior to wood and iron stocks for common use for all bower anchors. The hole in the crown for buoy rope or chain is drilled after the anchor is finished, and so is a check for bad

COMMANDER WILLIAM RODGER'S
PATENT DOUBLE-CONCAVE SMALL-PALMED ANCHOR.

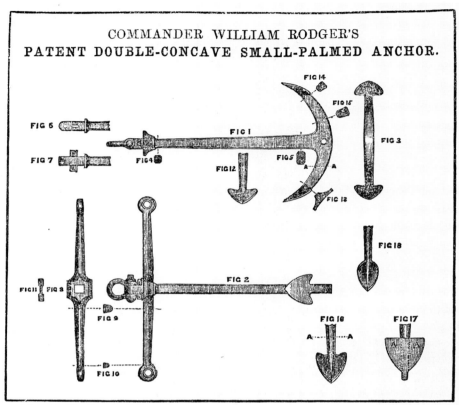

Drawn by WM. RODGER, R.N.

Fig. 1. A side view of the Patent Anchor, with the Stock in section.
,, 2. A plan of the same, stocked.
,, 3. A back view of the Crown, Arms and Palms.
,, 4 & 5. Sections of the Shank, taken at the dotted lines in Fig. 1.
,, 6 & 7. A side view and plan of the Square, without the stock, but shewing the Stock-key, Key-guide, and Key-hole.
,, 8. A back view of the Stock.
,, 9 & 10. Sections of the Stock, taken at the dotted lines in Figs. 2 & 8.
,, 11. A plan of the Stock-key-guide.
,, 12. A front view of the Arm and Palm.
,, 13. A Section of the Palm, taken at the dotted line in Fig. 1, and shewing its double-concave form.
,, 14 & 15. Sections of the Arm, shewing its wedge form.
,, 16. A front view of the Patent Palm, and part of the Arm, before it is bent.
,, 17. A front view of the large Palm, and part of the Arm, in common use, for an Anchor of the same weight as Figs. 1 and 2.
,, 18. A front view of the Arm, with a Palm suitable for Stream and Kedge Anchors which do not require to be "fished," and which Anchors are made considerably longer than the "Bowers" of the same weight.

NOTE.—The dotted lines A A, Figs. 1 & 16, indicate the position which the head of the large Palm in common use would assume if exhibited in those figures; and shows that the surfaces on the sides of the Arms of the Improved Anchor, are as great as that of the Corners A A, of the large Palm, Fig. 17, which loosens the ground in front; and if it be of an adhesive quality, causes the Anchor to become "shod." The Hole in the Crown is intended for the Buoy-Chain; and the Holes in the ends of the Stock are for the purpose of saving iron, where it would actually be in some degree, prejudicial to the holding of the Anchor.

Rodger's Patent Double-Concave Small-Palmed Anchor. (National Maritime Museum C6994)

An example of Rodger's Patent Double-Concave Small-Palmed Anchor from Canada. (National Defence Photo, by RCN)

workmanship in connecting arms with shank.

For *Stream* and *Kedge* anchors the stocks are oval in section and rove through the shank of the anchor with one end flat and a ring instead of a ball; the other end a bend with oval button rivetted on to the bent part so that the stock may be detached from the anchor if required.

The list of favourable testimonials is far too long to quote, ranging from HM Revenue cruisers off Tobermory; through the East India ship *Blenheim*, which bent links of the cable before starting the anchor; to *Alipore*, assailed by a violent gale going into Table Bay and unable to carry reefed topsails, when the anchor held without starting an inch . . . and many, many more alike.

To conclude, not only did the Lake Nemi anchor of about AD 40 resemble Lt Rodger's Pickaxe pattern: that found with the Danish ship at Ladby, and dated around AD 950 has a remarkable likeness to it. A length of chain cable about 30 feet long was attached to this anchor followed by rope leading to a windlass, proving an early understanding of the value of the catenary, while the length of the forerunner chain also minimised the danger of rope chafing against a typical rocky Scandinavian seabed.

Amongst his many gifts Lt Rodger appears to have had the knack of anticipating the future as well as reflecting the past. On St George's day in 1943 MV *Rowallan Castle* was commissioned for the Union Castle line, her load displacement being 15,715 tons. Her bower and spare bower anchors were Byers Stockless, but her stream anchor was a Rodger's anchor, as was that of the *Warwick Castle*. This impressive link between the early days of the Christian era and the recent past, over a period of 1900 years, is breathtaking.

George Cotsell and portable anchors

Halfway through the nineteenth century anchors were being developed by designers whose names seem to have been unfairly eclipsed. George Cotsell, Master Smith of Chatham Dockyard and High Constable of Gillingham 1859-60, was amongst these, following Pering in applying a scientific approach to the Royal Navy's anchor design. He published *A Treatise on Ships' Anchors* in 1856, at a time when there was a special concern with portable anchors, and his book gave a fine survey of these as well as other anchors.

At this time the term 'portable' was applied to anchors that could be dismantled in one of a number of ingenious ways. The advantages claimed were that such anchors, once disassembled, could be more easily carried out in the ship's boats, and could be conveniently stowed on board. Furthermore, most had

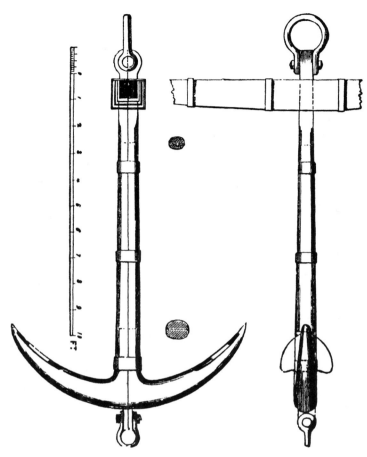

Captain Hall's Patent Portable Anchor could be divided longitudinally down the shank. (From George Cotsell's *A Treatise on Ships' Anchors*, 1856)

A model of Hutchen's Portable Anchor. (National Maritime Museum C8838/2a)

Portable anchors employed as mooring anchors: Hall's (top) and Cotsell's. (From George Cotsell's A Treatise on Ships' Anchors, 1856)

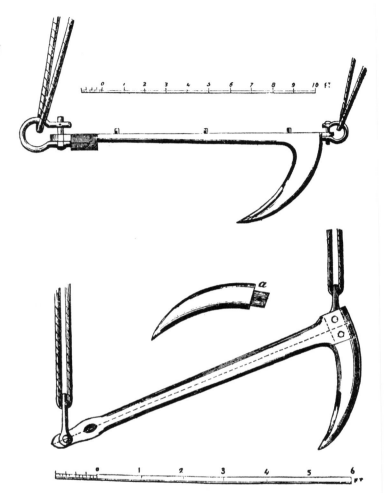

removable flukes, and some even divided into two down the shank, making them useful as light kedges, or as mooring anchors in shoal water (since there was no danger of the ship setting down on the upright fluke). Although they cost more initially, they could prove economical in the long run, because a broken fluke destroyed the whole value of a conventional anchor, whereas a 'portable' could replace the damaged half or fluke. The obvious disadvantage of the halved shank, however, was its inherent weakness, and if bent, it could not be reunited with the other half. This shortcoming inspired Cotsell's design.

His own portable anchor could have one arm removed; it was held on by a mortise and tenon type joint in the crown, with a hole to take a steel pin like the joint in anchor cables. John Hutchen's portable of 1846 was in three pieces, the crown and arms being in one, the shank in two. The shank was held together by three hoops and the anchor and buoy shackles. Captain Hall's, patented in 1840, was one divided down the shank from ring to crown. Lt Inglefield's, first exhibited at the Great Exhibition in 1851, had a partly rotating or moveable crown. Captain Dwyer's, designed about 1853, was of the Porter/Trotman type, with a crown that swivelled on the shank, and a device controlling the arc through which the arms could swing. Aylen's anchor resembled that of Lt Rodger's, as did Mitcheson's and Lenox's. A Mr Kington designed his hollow-shanked anchor around 1830; it had a tubular shank through which the cable passed, while a knot secured it in the bell-mouthed lower end. Hardly unexpected, it was unsuccessful, since its design suggests a confusion between the gunsmith's and anchormaker's arts. Morgan and Little's portable of 1832 could be broken down into eleven pieces, productive, no doubt, of some difficulty in remembering which went where.

In his *Treatise on Ships' Anchors* George Cotsell also included the forerunner of the modern stockless anchor, that designed by Mr R F Hawkins. To quote Cotsell:

> Many other attempts, at various times within the last fifty years, have been made to improve the anchor, and others again to supply anchors of a totally new character, as for instance, the patent anchor of Hawkins' construction, requiring no stock . . . both palms acting at the same time . . . with a tumbler acting crown and a tripping palm in its centre but not portable.

Before the stock disappears from the story of the anchor, it would be useful to summarise its own history in a separate chapter; but first it is necessary to look at parallel developments with iron cables and mooring chains.

Note: In full the dedication of his *Treatise* was 'To Admirals, Captains of His Majesty's Navy, the Hon. East India Company, Underwriters at Lloyds, the Society of Ship Owners . . . these observations are most respectfully submitted by their Very Obedient and Most Humble Servant . . . Richard Pering.'

10 | Chain cable and chains

In 1885 Thomas W Traill, CE, RN, Engineer Surveyor in Chief, Board of Trade, Inspector of Chain Cables and Anchor Proving Establishments, prefaced his *Chain Cables and Chains* with remarks on the difficulty of discovering any positive clues to their earliest manufacture and use. He made mention of 'King Solomon fetching Hiram, a worker in brass, out of Tyre, where he made wreaths of chains', but doubted that contemporary shipowners ever used chains in their vessels, and certainly not of brass. His reasonable conclusion was that the first iron chain cable was probably made in Britain and used in a ship flying the British flag. 'The art of making chain for cables, if ever known earlier, had to be acquired afresh.'

Moving forward in time, Traill noted that while a very large number of patents for making chain cables had been taken out, there were few actual advances towards improving their construction. Some here quoted give an impression of the patent situation from 1600 onwards.

In 1643 Phillip White, blacksmith, obtained a patent lasting fourteen years, costing him 'Five pounds in English money to be paid yearly to the Exchequer, Westminster, at the Feast of the Annuciation of the Blessed Virgin and St Michael the Archangel. For mooring purposes and cables.' His patent read: 'A way for the Mearing of Shipps with Yron Chaines by finding out the True Heating, Prepareing and Temping of Yron for that Purpose. And that he hath nowe attayned to the True Use of the said Chaynes, and that the same wilbe for the great Saveing of Cordage and Safety of Shippes, and will redound to the Good of our Comon Wealth.'

In 1690 Admiral Sir Cloudisley Shovell recommended that chain moorings should be introduced to the English service. Sadly, he did not live to further his ideas, being lost at sea when his ship the *Association* was wrecked off the Scillies in 1707.

In 1783 George Matthews of Broseley, Shropshire, patented a process for rendering various iron articles and chains 'malleable and tough as hammered or wrought iron'. He used an oven in which he spread charcoal over the article, then applied fire and excluded air allowing it to burn for 24 hours. The article remained in the oven until the charcoal had burnt out and the oven was perfectly cool.

In 1791 Colin Mackenzie patented a link and 'a certain method of making it which might be in his opinion useful for certain purposes, including mooring chains and ship's cables', but probably no ship's cable was made by this method, and the patent did not lessen the use of hempen cables.

From the early 1800s the names of significant men who designed cables and the ships which tested them come thick and fast, so it is impossible to detail every step on the way to the acceptance of chain cables. A chronological selection of those individuals and the tests which most advanced the use of chain now follows.

1804. An interesting entry: John Slater, surgeon of Huddersfield, Yorkshire, obtained a patent for 'A new improved method of making cables, shrouds, stays and other articles for the rigging of ships, of material never before used for that purpose . . . the substitution of metals for hemp, applied in the form of chainwork.' Note that the patent was solely for the application not the manufacture of materials used. In the same year William Hawks the Younger, iron manufacturer of Gateshead, obtained a patent for improvements in making chains for use in mines and other purposes.

1808. A more detailed account of the use of chain cables at sea is needed here. The *Ann & Isabella* of 220 tons, built at Berwick on Tweed, carried a chain cable made by Robert Flinn, son of a soldier of General Wolfe's army and with him when he fell at Quebec. The young Robert was brought up as a blacksmith by his uncle at Ford Forge on the River Till, Northumberland. He was an ingenious and expert workman, having at one time the monopoly of harpoons for the whale

Brown twist-link chain cable, with and without studs. (From Thomas Traill's *Chain Cables and Chains, 1885*)

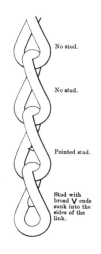

No stud.

No stud.

Pointed stud.

Stud with broad **V** ends sunk into the sides of the link.

fishery. Traill considered him the finest artificer of chain cables in his generation. The iron used for *Ann & Isabella*'s cable was rectangular and worked into round by hand hammer on an anvil; it was not fitted with studs. Later in the year the same cable saved a whole tier of ships made fast to *Ann & Isabella*, their hempen cables having been cut by floating ice in the flooded River Tyne.

This year also saw an early mention of an important name in cable-making. Samuel Brown, then a lieutenant in the Royal Navy, and later Sir Samuel, obtained a patent for 'certain improvements and inventions in the rigging and equipage of ships'. The latter included chains for cables, to be made of short twisted links. He also proposed swivels and shifting shackles at the anchor rings, for slipping the anchor if necessary, a very important function since a chain cable could not be cut in an emergency. Traill considered this patent the first incontrovertible step towards making chain cable a success. The importance of Brown's name is underlined by Traill; noting that Brown, Lenox were still making chains and cables, and had done so before any company 'now in existence' (*ie* in 1885).

1811. By this time very favourable reports on the new material, Samuel Brown's included, were reaching the Admiralty. At the Nore anchorage in HMS *Namur* with Brown on board, Admiral Sir Henry Stanhope conducted very searching and extensive tests of her iron cables to, as the Navy put it, his entire satisfaction. As a result the Navy Board, wary as usual of new ideas, now formed a committee of officers to consider the new cables. Further trials of Brown's cables concentrated on their use in stationary ships of the Navy in open roadsteads, which suggests that it was the regular handling of chain aboard sea-going ships that was the chief cause of official reservations.

1812. On receiving a report from HM Naval Transport *Aid* that she rode out gales in the Downs more easily with the iron cables than with the hemp, the Board ordered three cables for the Transports *Assistance*, *Portsmouth* and *Chatham*.

1813. By the following year Brown was making cables at Millwall on the Thames; he improved them by side-welding the links, and fitting studs. He also designed a Proving Machine.

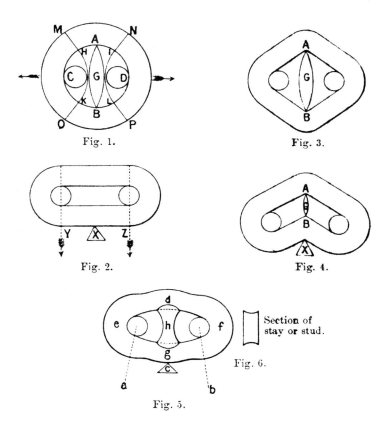

Fig. 1.

Fig. 3.

Fig. 2.

Fig. 4.

Fig. 5.

Section of stay or stud.

Fig. 6.

Brunton's experiments to establish the best form of link for chain cables. (From Thomas Traill's Chain Cables and Chains, 1885)

This year was also significant for the obtaining of a patent by Brown's great rival and advocate of stud links, Thomas Brunton of Cooper's Row, Crutched Friars, London; this was for improvements in chain cables and moorings. He also produced theories on suitable links; various types were analysed, and the rivalry between the two men took the form of disputes over studs and twisted links, Brown later adopting the former and discontinuing the latter. He did not look as far back as the North of England men for support of his opinions – the latter, to support their opposition to Brunton's patent, advanced the claim that studded links had been used in King Solomon's time: it is not known what evidence they produced to clinch this! Brunton allowed himself to be diverted from his 'paper war' with Samuel Brown to bring and win a lawsuit against William Hawks Senior & Co who were making stud-link cables.

Testing machines were increasingly in use in this period;

with such advances in the manufacture of chain it was obvious that proving of the product had become essential.

1814. By this year the demand for chain cable had increased enormously. The brigantine *Kent* was built at Deptford for the Baltic trade, supervised by Phillip Laing's Foreman, Laing being an eminent Northeast shipbuilder. She was fitted with chain cable made at Sunderland from iron forged by Sir Edward Crawley out of scrap metal. The links' ends were welded and studs were fitted. Two sorts of studs were available, defined as 'Lady' or 'Gentleman' studs according to the size of waist (the workman appears to have amused himself at work then as now).

Phillip Laing was an early advocate of iron cables. Looking ahead to 1823 the brig rigged vessel *Vesper*, which he built on the River Wear, was completely fitted with these, in all a total of 190 fathoms. A percipient man, he had observed fishermen riding out gales with stones attached along their hemp cables, and appreciated how this extra weight allowed their boats to ride more easily. Two years later his ships were no longer supplied with any hemp cables.

1815. By now the merchant service had so far accepted iron cables that when carried, they were noted in the ship's records with her other particulars. The ship rigged vessel *Nautilus*,

Elements of a stud-link cable: E - anchor shackle; B - end link; C - enlarged link; D common links; S - studs. (From Thomas Traill's Chain Cables and Chains, *1885)*

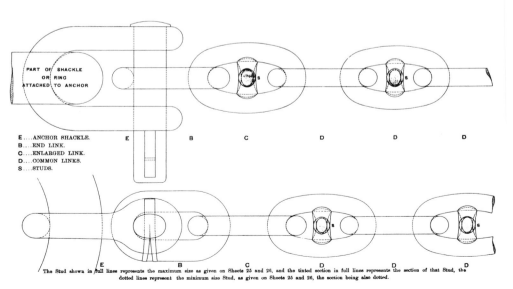

PART OF SHACKLE OR RING ATTACHED TO ANCHOR

E....ANCHOR SHACKLE.
B....END LINK.
C....ENLARGED LINK.
D....COMMON LINKS.
S....STUDS.

The Stud shown in full lines represents the maximum size as given on Sheets 25 and 26, and the tinted section in full lines represents the section of that Stud, the dotted lines represent the minimum size Stud, as given on Sheets 25 and 26, the section being also dotted.

built at Chepstow in 1800, probably had all chain cables by this year.

During the Napoleonic Wars it became obvious that some French vessels were fitted with chain cables. A French privateer taken as prize by a British man-of-war had them, probably supplied by Brunton through his connections across the channel, as her cables' links were apparently typical of his design. These connections included some support from the French government.

1817. Chain cable manufacture was now carried on at Bristol by Griffiths and Lewis. They had at first made grates and small chains, but went from the domestic to the marine market, and later made cables for the *Great Western*, the first British steamer to cross the Atlantic. They followed this by supplying the cables for the *Great Britain*, the largest vessel of the time.

1819. Duncan McDougall made cables with a stud link; the last made by him was for a 'nobleman's' yacht, its name unfortunately not known. Traill wrote that 'None of McDougall's cables were ever known to have parted; many makers of the present day [1885] would be pleased to be able to state as much'. It is very probable that makers of cables of this present day [1999] would be equally pleased to state the same.

1820. In this year the chain trade in South Staffordshire received an unexpected boost thanks to Noah Hingley. While small chain-making round Dudley had been flourishing, Hingley now contracted with a Liverpool shipowner to make a chain cable to replace hemp: 'Its size to be 1½ inches', exceptionally large at that time, and totally new to the workmen. The links were end-welded, with studs, the ends of the latter made hollow, and to fit the inner sides of the links. The workmen after a few trials succeeded in producing a good cable in 15-fathom lengths. This attracted attention and orders from far and wide, and a day's holiday was awarded to celebrate the event.

A highly energetic man, often riding from Dudley to Liverpool instead of travelling by coach, Hingley was also active in promoting the use of steam hammers; with James Nasmyth he was the first to erect one in the district.

1823. This year a Trinity House Light Vessel was moored with iron cables for the first time, and the East India Company's vessels were also supplied with them. Other shipowners were greatly encouraged by this, adding to the already considerable demand for iron cables.

However, after this date chain-making on the Thames gradually ceased: it was less costly to manufacture in the North, where the iron was forged and coal was cheaper than in London.

The introduction of chain required changes to the traditional methods of handling cables. This manual of seamanship demonstrates some of the earliest modifications: to the whelps of the windlass (Fig 11); a roller at the hawse hole (Fig 12); and a cable stopper (Figs 13 and 14). (From Darcy Lever's Young Sea Officer's Sheet Anchor, *1819)*

Diameter of Chain substituted for Small Ropes in Merchant Ships, and Acraman's Average Proof-strain on the Chains, from Hedderwick, 1830

Girth of Rope Inches	Diameter of Chain Inches	Proof-strain with cross-bars Tons	Proof-strain without cross-bars Tons Cwt	
2	$^3/_{16}$	1	0	15
3	$^5/_{16}$	1	0	18
4	$^3/_8$	2	1	15
$4^3/_4$	$^7/_{16}$	3	2	15

NOTE. The diameter of chain substituted for larger ropes or cables, also the proof-strain, will be found in their respective columns in the table in Chapter 7.

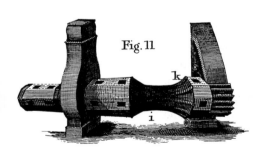

Fig. 11

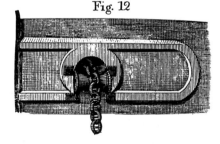

Fig. 12

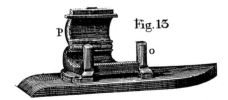

Fig. 13

Fig. 14

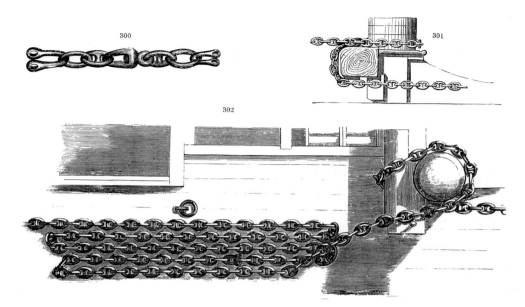

The Royal Navy and Chain Cables

In 1814, after an iron cable had been on trial for more than a year in HM Transport *Assistance*, the Commander's final report on it, after some initial doubts, was most favourable. Amongst other comments he wrote that the iron cable had held in a severe gale off the Scillies with one anchor only, while other vessels with hemp cables and two anchors down drove ashore.

The year 1816 saw a cautious advance in their use, limited to supplying one each to sloops and smaller vessels on the home station. But there was a considerable change in 1817: one and a half chain cables were to be supplied to all sea-going ships of the Fifth Rate and upwards, and one to all Sixth Rates and sloops. In 1823 there was further progress: all sloops of 14 and 10 guns were now allotted two chain cables instead of one; 28-gun vessels and brigs carrying 18 guns were also allowed two, and frigates were in future to have two instead of one and a half. By this increased allowance every ship in the British Service had two chain cables. As Traill remarked, it cannot be said that iron cables were hurriedly adopted into the Royal Navy.

Five years later brigs and sloops had their allowance of chain cables increased from two to three, but no alterations were made as to the hempen cable allowance–a belt-and-braces

Bitts reinforced for use with chain cables. The detail (top right) shows a chain swivel. (From George Nares' Seamanship, 1883 edition)

policy possibly deferring to old prejudice. It took three years more for the next major step. In 1831 vessels in the British Service were to be supplied as follows: First to Sixth Rates to carry four chain cables; sloops and cutters two. Numbers of hempen cables were much reduced.

It was, in fact, about twenty-one years since chain cables had been experimentally tested in HMS *Crescent*, a typically cautious approach by the Board of Admiralty. The days of hemp cables, as Traill remarked, were finally numbered when the full allocation of chain cables in accordance with the number of anchors, was supplied to all vessels in the Royal Navy. For these a testing machine was first made in Dockyards, at Woolwich in 1833 and three more at Plymouth.

From these iron cables, new in the 1800s, the way was already opening towards production of the heavy steel cables that now restrain at anchor the very largest vessels afloat today. Thomas Traill, it must not be forgotten, concluded his account with severe criticisms of unscrupulous manufacturers of the new cables, and the disasters caused by their breakage. From these he exempted Bridport in Dorset, 'famed worldwide for honourable dealing and good hemp cables.' Sadly, this works has now finally closed.

One long-term advantage of the chain cable was that even the largest sizes could be brought directly to the capstan once a suitable drum had been devised. This is a Brown Patent with a form of sprocket wheel which fitted the links of the cables. (From George Nares' *Seamanship, 1883* edition)

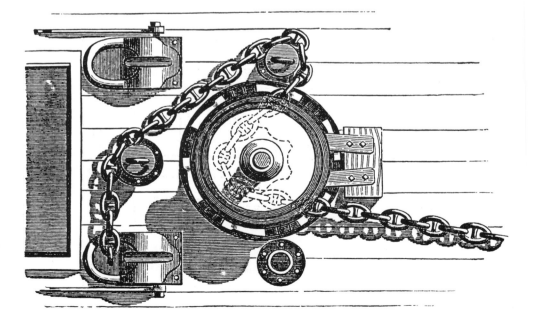

Size of Hawse-holes, with the Weight and Size of Cables for each Class of Ships, from Fincham, 1825

			HEMPEN CABLES.													CHAIN CABLES.												
			Bower, &c.		Stream.	Weight of each Cable.						Hawse-holes.			Bower.		Stream.		Weight of the Quantity supplied.						Hawse-holes.		
						Bower.			Stream.			Thickness of Lead Pipe.		Hawse-hole in the Clear.					Bower.			Stream.			Thickness of Pipes.		Hawse-hole in the Clear.
			No.	Size.	Size.							Upp. Part.	Lower Part.		Quantity.	Size.	Quantity.	Size.							Lead.	Iron.	
	Guns.	Tons.		in.	in.	Cwt.	qr.	lb.	Cwt.	qr.	lb.	in.	in.	in.	Fath.	in.	Fath.	in.	Cwt.	qr.	lb.	Cwt.	qr.	lb.	in.	in.	in.
Three-deck Ships..	120		5	25	14	122	1	19	38	1	25	½	1¼	19½	150	2⅛	100	1⅜	326	3	13	90	3	27	¼	1¼	19½
	110		5	25	14	122	1	19	38	1	25	½	1¼	19½	150	2⅛	100	1⅜	326	3	13	90	3	27	¼	1¼	19½
	104		5	24	14	112	2	25	38	1	25	½	1¼	19	150	2⅛	100	1¼	326	3	13	75	0	8	¼	1¼	19
	98		5	23	13½	103	2	12	35	3	2	½	1¼	18	150	2⅛	100	1¼	326	3	13	75	0	8	¼	1¼	18
Two-deck Ships....	86		5	23	13½	103	2	14	35	3	2	½	1¼	18	150	2⅛	100	1¼	326	3	13	75	0	8	¼	1¼	18
	84		5	23	13½	103	2	14	35	3	2	½	1¼	18	150	2⅛	100	1¼	326	3	13	75	0	8	¼	1¼	18
	82		5	23	13½	103	2	14	35	3	2	½	1¼	18	150	2⅛	100	1¼	326	3	13	75	0	8	¼	1¼	18
	80		5	23	13½	103	2	14	35	3	2	½	1¼	18	150	2⅛	100	1¼	326	3	13	75	0	8	¼	1¼	18
	78		5	23	13½	103	2	14	35	3	2	½	1¼	18	150	2⅛	100	1¼	326	3	13	75	0	8	¼	1¼	18
	76		5	23	13½	103	2	14	35	3	2	½	1¼	18	150	2⅛	100	1¼	326	3	13	75	0	8	¼	1¼	18
	74		5	22	13	94	2	0	33	0	8	½	1¼	17	150	2	100	1¼	290	3	27	75	0	8	¼	1⅛	17
	58		5	19	11½	70	2	4	25	2	16	½	1¼	14½	150	1⅞	100	1⅛	255	1	7	60	2	26	¼	1⅛	14½
Frigate Class.......	60		5	21	13	86	0	7	33	0	8	½	1¼	16	200	1⅞	100	1⅛	340	1	18	60	2	26	¼	1⅛	16
	50		5	18	11	63	0	12	23	2	14	½	1¼	14	200	1¾	100	1⅛	296	0	8	60	2	26	¼	1	14
	48		5	18	11	63	0	12	23	2	14	½	1¼	14	200	1¾	100	1⅛	296	0	8	60	2	26	¼	1	14
	46		5	17½	11	59	2	26	23	2	14	½	1¼	13½	200	1¾	100	1⅛	296	0	8	60	2	26	¼	1	13½
	44		5	17½	11	59	2	26	23	2	14	½	1¼	13½	200	1¾	100	1⅛	296	0	8	60	2	26	¼	1	13½
	42		5	17½	11	59	2	26	23	2	14	½	1¼	13½	200	1¾	100	1⅛	296	0	8	60	2	26	¼	1	13½
	34		5	14½	9	41	0	19	15	3	12	½	1¼	12	200	1⅝	100	⅞	181	3	26	36	2	13	¼	⅞	12
	32		5	14½	9	41	0	19	15	3	12	½	1¼	12	200	1⅝	100	⅞	181	3	26	36	2	13	¼	⅞	12
	28		4	14½	9	41	0	19	15	3	12	½	1¼	12	200	1⅝	100	⅞	181	3	26	36	2	13	¼	⅞	12
	26		4	14½	9	41	0	19	15	3	12	½	1¼	12	200	1⅝	100	⅞	181	3	26	36	2	13	¼	⅞	12
Flush-deck........	20	450	4	14½	9	41	0	19	15	3	12	½	1¼	12	200	1⅝	100	⅞	181	3	26	36	2	13	¼	⅞	12
	18	460	4	13½	7½	35	3	2	10	3	5	½	1¼	10¼	200	1½	100	¾	150	0	16	26	3	13	¼	⅞	10¼
	18	400	4	13½	7½	35	3	2	10	3	5	½	1¼	10¼	200	1½	100	¾	150	0	16	26	3	13	¼	⅞	10¼
	18	382	4	13½	7½	35	3	2	10	3	5	½	1¼	10¼	200	1½	100	¾	150	0	16	26	3	13	¼	⅞	10¼
	16	255	4	13½	7½	35	3	2	10	3	5	½	1¼	10¼	200	1½	100	¾	150	0	16	26	3	13	¼	⅞	10¼
	10	235	4	11	6½	23	2	14	8	0	11	⅜	1⅛	9½	200	1⅛	100	11–16	121	1	24	23	0	0	¼	¾	9½
Cutter	10	160	0	10	6½	19	2	8	8	0	11	⅜	⅞	8	300	1	100	11–16	142	2	23	23	0	0	¼	¾	8

* When commanded by a Lieutenant, has three chain Cables and no hempen.

11 | *Anchor stocks*

In earlier chapters anchor stocks have been considered with the anchors of which they were a part. This chapter contains more detailed notes on their materials and proportions and mainly refers to those stocks sited in the conventional position at the upper end of the shank.

During the centuries preceding the invention of stockless anchors, the purpose of the anchor stock was well understood. Fitted at a right-angle to the plane of the arms, it turned the anchor into a position where the flukes (at the end of the arms) dug into the sea bed. Lying more or less flat there, it could sink to some extent in a soft holding ground and add to the grip of the arms. Lead stocks, or wooden stocks with lead inset, increased the anchor's weight and its holding power, and this effect was further enhanced at a much later date when chain cables replaced hemp.

Anchors with stocks were represented from earliest times: on coins of the era of the Persian Emperor Darius, *circa* 500 BC. They were also shown on Thracian coins of about 400 BC, although the Thracians had no fleet in the fourth and fifth cen-

A Roman lead stock. (National Maritime Museum C6754/16)

Model of a Chinese junk anchor with a stock at the crown. (National Maritime Museum C8838/23a)

turies BC. They were also shown on murals, like that in the tomb of Flavius Rufinus, in the Catacombs at Rome, from around the start of the first century AD. Most notably, the famous mosaic in the House of Tycho, the Casa di Ancora in Pompeii and dating from the end of the first century BC, illustrates perfectly the traditional stocked anchor. All the above show the stock fitted in the familiar position, at the upper end of the shank.

Stocks have also been sited, less commonly, at the crown of the anchor – the following are examples:

(**a**) The bow anchor of the Chinese ship *Keying*. This vessel sailed from Hong Kong to London via New York in 1848. Her 'stock' was of bamboo rods which were passed through the crown of the anchor, and lashed into place. It should be noted that Dr Moll in his article on the anchor of 1927 considered there was a resemblance to a native Malayan anchor, but this seems unlikely. It is possible that a drawing was misinterpreted.

(**b**) A model of a Chinese junk anchor. The arms are at an acute angle, bound with iron bands and chocks are placed between these and the crown to prevent the bands slipping towards the crown. The stock is at the crown, and runs between the flukes

Model of an anchor with a frame stock, 1829. (National Maritime Museum C8837/37a)

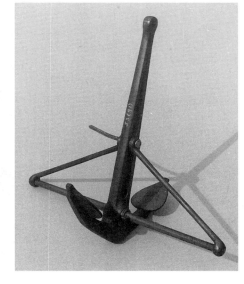

Model of a Brown's Patent Anchor, 1894. (National Maritime Museum C8818/28)

Moving from Chinese to Western anchors, the following designs also place the stock at the crown end of the shank:

(**c**) An anchor of around 1829 has a frame stock, with the stock passing through the crown at right-angles to the arms and close to them.

(**d**) A stockless anchor has a swivelling 'stock' rocking between the fork at the crown, the curved arms running through the fork; there is a ring on the crown. This anchor resembles a design by Hawkins of 1821.

(**e**) Brown's Patent Anchor of around 1894. The metal stock passes through the shank near the crown, with a pair of arms pivoted on to the stock on either side of the shank.

Proportions of Stocks

The Gokstad ship's anchor stock; it was essentially round in cross-section. (From Carl V Sølver, Om Ankre, 1945)

The stock of the Gokstad ship of around AD 850 and excavated in 1896 in Oslo Fjord, was unusually long, but in later centuries stocks became closer in size to parts of the anchors them-

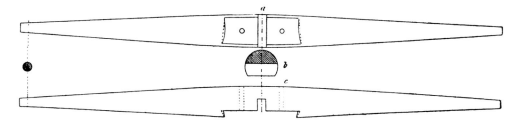

selves. Proportions changed little between 1600 and 1815. Sir Henry Mainwaring's *Seamen's Dictionary* of 1622 stated: 'The shank should be three times as long as one of the flukes, and the anchors proportionate to the tonnage of the ship.' The stock was the same length as the shank. The Pering round-crown type introduced a shorter stock, but later nineteenth-century stocks, both of wood and iron, were usually equal to the length of the shank; *eg*, around 1825 the length was equal to the length of the shank plus half the diameter of the ring.

The construction of an Admiralty stock demonstrated by the disintegration of this recovered example. (Author)

Materials – Wood

The wooden stocks of the Admiralty type during the eighteenth and nineteenth centuries were made in two horizontal halves of best oak held together by bands driven over and bolted. Usually there were three bands a side on large anchors over two tons and two bands on smaller. In some early anchors treenails (*ie* wooden dowels) were used in place of bolts, and later both were combined. The two sections could have an opening between them at the shank of about ½ to 1¼ inches with a chock about 3 inches wide placed between them, and any slack taken up by driving the bands further on. There were iron collar pieces round the hole for the shank to reduce wear.

These wooden stocks were straight on the top, tapered on either side and on the underside. The ends were square until about 1780, then rounded to avoid damage to the hull's copper sheathing. Wooden stocks remained in use aboard naval vessels with timber hulls; even up to 1856 anchors over three tons had wooden stocks, although the iron stock was reintroduced for smaller sizes at the end of the eighteenth century.

Materials – Iron

Iron stocks, after being used in the first century AD, went out of favour until about 1800. It was then reintroduced in small anchors and more generally used in the Royal Navy as the century progressed. The Admiralty iron stock was held in place by a shoulder piece on one side of the shank, and a forelock on the

Fig. 1.   Admiralty *Wood* Stock.

Fig. 2.   Lieut. Rodger's *Wood* Stock.

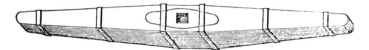

Fig. 3.   Admiralty *Iron* Stock.

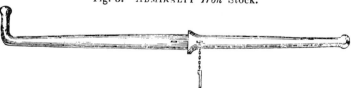

Fig. 4.   Lieut. Rodger's *Iron* Stock.

The nineteenth-century development of stocks from wood to iron in various patent forms. (From George Cotsell's *A Treatise on Ships' Anchors*, 1856)

Fig. 5.   Cotsell's *Iron* Stock.

other. George Cotsell designed a stock with a key that fitted
into a matching keyway in the hole in the stock provided for the
shank. A steel pin through shank and stock was held in place
with a lead pellet that prevented it from dropping out.

Before the discovery of the Nemi anchor, Captain Rodger,
RN had been credited with the invention of moveable stocks, his
design having been exhibited in the Great Exhibition of 1851.
After the Nemi anchor was raised, moveable stocks were
claimed as a Roman invention. Julius Caesar's own remarks
about the Veneti in his *De Bello Gallico* seems to disprove this
and return the credit to more northerly seafarers.

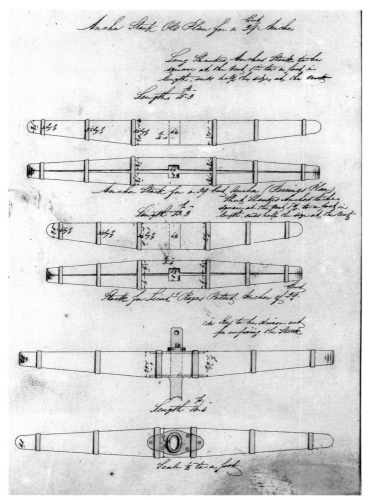

*Official draught
comparing anchor stocks
for a 39 hundredweight
anchor: (top) traditional
pattern, length 15 feet 3
inches; (centre) Pering's
plan, length 13 feet 3
inches; (bottom) Rodger's
Patent, length 16 feet 4
inches.* (National
Maritime Museum
DR7694)

12 | *The stockless anchor*

Hawkins and Martin patterns

In 1821 R F Hawkins, patenting his anchor, remarked:

> Its advantages are many, and all arise from the anchor being so constructed that both the flukes (which act on a revolving principle) penetrate into the ground at the same time. The consequences are: first that it holds therefore nearly equal to two anchors. Second, that it will not foul or cut, chafe or injure the cable. Third, that it does not require a stock. Fourth, that it breaks ground much easier, and is more con-

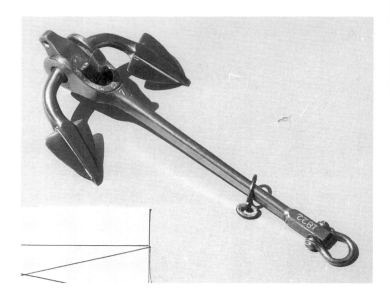

A model of Hawkins Patent Stockless, 1821; a pioneering design and the ancestor of all later stockless anchors.
(National Maritime Museum C8818/24)

The working of the Hawkins Anchor. (From a contemporary brochure)

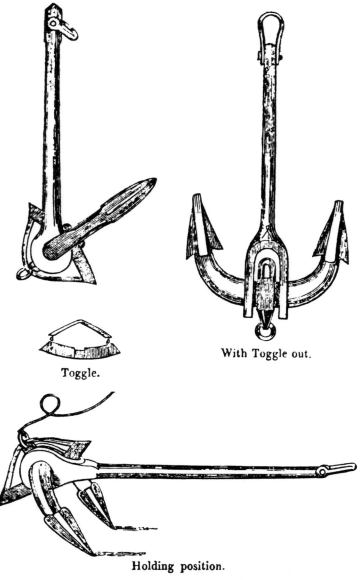

Toggle.

With Toggle out.

Holding position.

veniently worked; does not impede the way of the vessel in being hove up . . . will stow without any projection, can never injure the bows in weighing, catting or fishing, and is particularly adapted for kedging . . . and fifth, that in the event of a ship grounding upon her anchor her bottom cannot be injured, which is often the case with the common anchor.

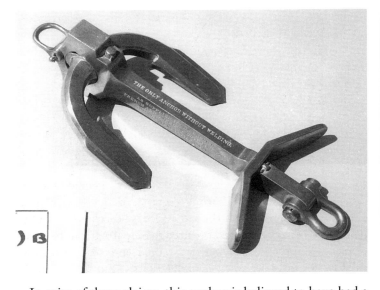

The Martin's Anchor in operation. (From George Nares' *Seamanship*, 1883 edition)

In spite of these claims, this anchor is believed to have had a tendency to fall over sideways, and the obvious and now universal advantages must seem to have been outweighed by this, or possibly reluctance by shipowners and the Admiralty to break away from proven designs. It was the most radical innovation in anchor design for centuries, and one authority has suggested that it was developed before the maritime world was ready to receive it. Whatever the reason, Hawkins's design was a first step from the old and laborious system of 'catting and fishing', particularly in the case of the Trotman anchor, towards the modern stockless anchor. According to Cotsell: 'It

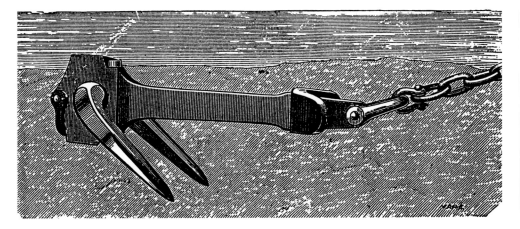

would appear that the anchor was not extensively patronised and has fallen into disuse.'

On the other hand François Martin's Patent Self-Canting Anchor, transitional between the Admiralty pattern and the more modern stockless anchors, was accepted. It was assembled from three forged sections, without welds, and in 1862 received an International Exhibition Prize Medal in London. Although Martin's London agent claimed in its publicity that it had no stock, it actually had a short one for stabilising in the same plane as the arms. This same agent, apart from his not unreasonable tendency to puff his client's designs, claimed amongst others the advantages of 'having no stock . . . with both flukes engaged in the ground at the same time, it can neither foul or be fouled; being composed of three main parts it can be taken to pieces and easily stowed away; being lighter than any other anchor, labour is greatly lessened by its use.' Finally his clinching factor: 'It is the cheapest of all others, where the quality of the material is equally good, and taking into account the difference in weight.'

This anchor was first manufactured by Gateshead Ironworks about 1859, and was demonstrated that year to the Bretheren

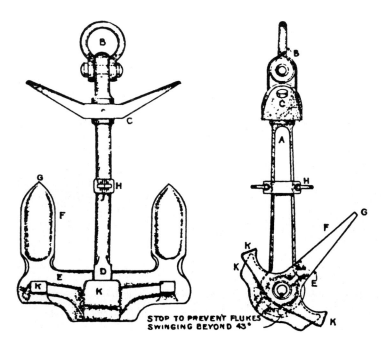

STOP TO PREVENT FLUKES
SWINGING BEYOND 43°

The improved Martin's Close-Stowing Anchor, with tripping palms (k). (From the Admiralty Anchor Book of 1892)

of Trinity House, Newcastle-upon-Tyne, who granted their certificate, declaring their conviction of 'its astonishing superiority over all those in present use.' In December 1863 an official trial took place in Woolwich Dockyard, in the presence of Sir Frank Nicholson, senior Naval officers, the Master Shipwright and Martin himself, plus at least five representatives of newspapers. One of the latter reported, 'The trial's results proved the superiority of the anchor over those used at present in the Royal Navy.' In 1864 it was approved by the Admiralty, and patented. The only suggestion for subsequent improvement made was that a larger shackle be fitted before it was issued for trials at sea. There were certain reservations about the stowage: 'the anchor has been catted and fished, and it was found that owing to its peculiar shape some different arrangements will be required for stowing it at sea.'

It proved generally popular in the Navy: its flukes did not impede the firing of guns in an ironclad, nor project over the side when ramming, nor above the ground when on the bot-

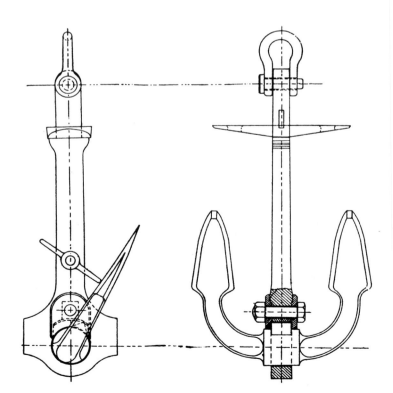

Wright's Improved Martin Self-Canting Anchor, sanctioned by Lloyd's 24 November 1892. (Lloyd's Register of Shipping)

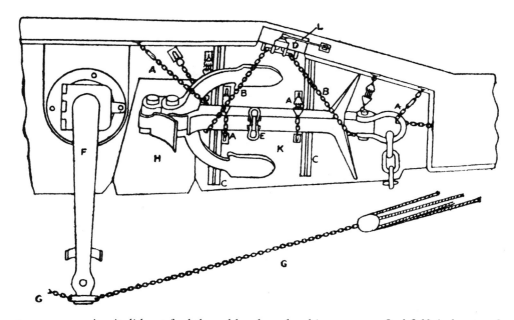

Inglefield Anchor stowed on a bed. (From the Admiralty *Manual of Seamanship* of 1915)

tom, so ensuring it did not foul the cable when the ship swung. It remained in service until after the Second World War as a kedge anchor in small craft, and as such was used to haul vessels off the invasion beaches.

As improved by Wright, Martin's Self-Canting Anchor was sanctioned by Lloyd's in 1892. A later Martin's Stockless Anchor of around 1906 had a squarer shaped crown, and tripping palms at the base of each fluke.

While the foregoing refers almost entirely to the naval adoption of the Martin's anchor, the Board of Trade investigated the possibility of its use in passenger ships. There was much disagreement between Liverpool Underwriters and Lloyd's Register about allowances for weight reduction for anchors of this type. Finally the Board of Trade instructed surveyors that if Lloyd's Rules on weight and size of anchors were complied with, the question of efficiency would not be raised.

Similar patterns were now being produced, one by Admiral Inglefield, once the lieutenant of that name, now presumably long promoted. An even later Improved Martin's Type model came out in 1966, sixty years after Martin's Improved Unchokeable Anchor appeared.

From about 1860 anchor 'beds' on the ship's focsle were used as stowage and launching devices for close-stowing anchors. These 'beds' were inclined, to give the anchor a start. Stocked anchors also were launched from this type of 'bed'.

The complicated method of securing this anchor to its vertical 'bed' finally led to its general disuse, as catting and fishing had disappeared earlier. By the late 1800s many patterns of stockless anchors, where the shank was drawn up to the hawse hole shaped for it in the ship's side, had been proposed.

It is not unlikely that, just as the Hawkins anchor appeared too early for its acceptance by the maritime world, the Martin's anchor suffered by being produced too late; the tide of new stockless designs simply washed over it.

The triumph of the stockless anchor

Cathead anchor stowage, needing large numbers to handle it, had disappeared. It was succeeded by the many patterns of stockless anchors, with tilting flukes, and a shank drawn up into

Early Hall 'Unchokeable' Anchor with stock. (Vosper Thornycroft)

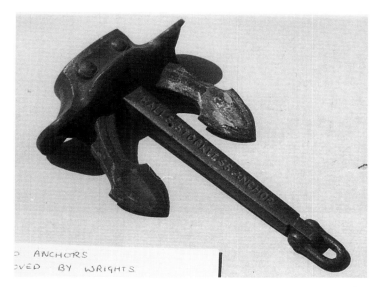

the hawse hole shaped for it in the ship's side. With the aid of a powered capstan or windlass this type could probably be worked with three seamen when anchoring, and about twice that number when weighing.

It is possible to believe that hawse holes, now in use for anchor cables and anchor stowage, may owe their origin to the pair of eyes painted on the bows of ancient ships to assist them in finding their way over uncharted waters. It has been suggested that the word 'hawse' might be traced back to the Old English word 'hals', meaning neck, *ie* holes in the 'neck' of the ship. This word seems hardly used much before 1600, when the anchor was usually stowed on the gunwale or the channels.

Returning to the modern stockless anchor, in the late 1800s Lloyd's sanctioned the anchors now being produced by well-known names, foreign as well as British. Hall's, one of the best known, introduced their stockless anchor in 1886. The head of this anchor was held by a pin through it, the pin in turn held by 'keeps' inserted in the head. The next step was an improvement of this by Wright, followed by Hall's Improved Patent Anchor. Noah Hingley & Sons were responsible for it, the company already familiar to the reader as manufacturers of chain cable (Chapter 10).

This anchor was sanctioned by Lloyd's in 1923, and rapidly became one of the most popular of the period. Henry Bessemer

Hall's Improved Patent Anchor, 1923: the National Maritime Museum's example, from the Union Castle Line. (National Maritime Museum C4076/3)

had taken out a patent for cast steel anchors, but it was not until Hall's Improved Patent Anchor appeared that the new material came into general use for anchor manufacture. This new Hall's anchor, on display in the National Maritime Museum

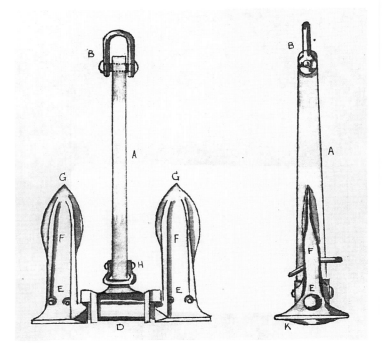

Wasteney Smith Patent Anchor, as carried in the pre-dreadnought battleship Hindustan *in 1908.* (From a contemporary manuscript)

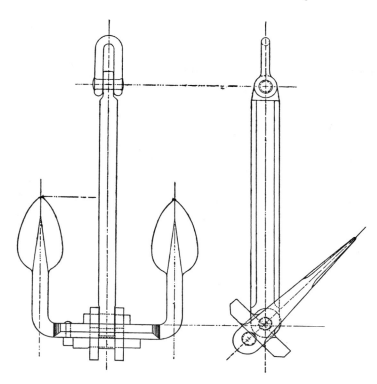

Samuel Taylor & Sons'
1892 pattern stockless
anchor. (Lloyd's
Register of Shipping)

anchor park, was until 1977 the spare anchor for the Union
Castle mail ships based at Southampton. It was essential to prevent delay to the sailing of any mail vessel that had lost an
anchor in service. It now commemorates the men of this service, to South Africa from Britain, over 120 years.

In 1886 Wasteney Smith also produced one of the first
stockless anchors, with shank and crosshead being in one piece.
The two arms were keyed on each end of a large pin which
passed through the crosshead, working freely within it; the
arms were held from revolving beyond 45 degrees either way.
Modification of this type resulted in Wasteney's E Type, and
further improvements produced the F Type, approved in 1918.

Samuel Taylor's anchor of 1892 was followed by their
famous 'Dreadnought' anchor. It was sanctioned by Lloyd's in
1909, and an improved model in 1927. Like Hall's, it became
one of the most popular anchors of the period. The other
Samuel, Baxter, was less successful with his anchors. He met
with little encouragement from the Royal Navy, but the
Brazilian Navy specified his 1882 design for the turret ships

*A model of Taylor's
1909 pattern
'Dreadnought' stockless
anchor.* (National
Maritime Museum
C8820/18)

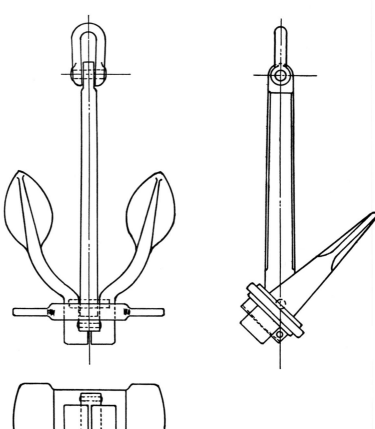

*The Modified
'Dreadnought' Anchor,
sanctioned 11 April
1927.* (Lloyd's
Register of Shipping)

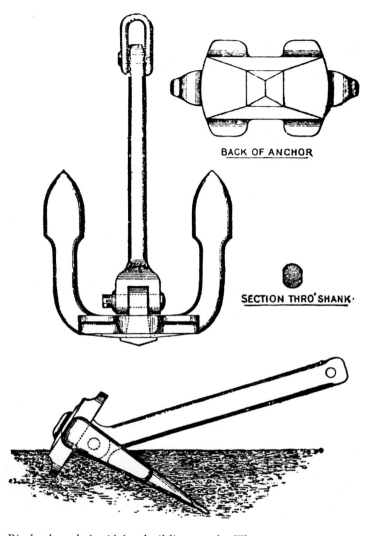

BACK OF ANCHOR

SECTION THRO'SHANK·

A contemporary magazine illustration of the Byers 'Reliance' Stockless Anchor of 1890.

Riachuelo and *Aquidaban* building on the Thames.

W L Byers of Sunderland developed stockless anchors over a period in the late nineteenth century. His first was patented in 1887; in 1890 the inner surface of the flukes was made concave to improve its holding power. The inclined fins for tripping were patented in 1900.

W L Byers himself was widely read, and fascinated by the discoveries made by Heinrich Schliemann at the supposed site of Troy. His correspondence with the latter records that he had named his ships after Homeric heroes, and cast into his company's anchors (and adopted as his house flag) the swastika device from pottery excavated at Troy. This led to an interesting enquiry from a retired Marine Chief Engineer in Montevideo. An anchor with the swastika device had been retrieved from the River Plate, and the National Maritime Museum was asked if this could have been carried in the *Graf Spee*, the German 'pocket battleship' scuttled there in 1939. Unfortunately for the Chief Engineer, founder of his own small maritime museum, this was impossible, as 'W L Byers Sunderland' was cast into the shank.

A Byers Stockless Anchor, with prominent swastikas on the flukes, recovered from the River Plate. (Museo Maritimo, Montevideo)

The 190 hundredweight Byers Improved Stockless Anchor from HMS Ark Royal. (Author)

A Byers Improved Stockless Anchor, weighing 190 hundred-weight is in the care of the National Maritime Museum. It is one of the two main anchors carried in HMS *Ark Royal*, the Royal Navy's last conventional aircraft carrier, which went to the breakers in 1980.

Of the foreign anchor manufacturers the Baldt Anchor Company had a stockless anchor sanctioned in 1898; this, and the Canadian Steel Foundries anchor of 1908 both offered notable competition to the British makers. The Bayer Stockless was patented in 1887, and further developed in 1900. In the early 1920s French, Italian, German, Dutch and even Japanese had entered the market, their anchors having been sanctioned by Lloyd's – indeed, the 1945 Lloyd's pattern book of approved designs includes eighty-seven models, the vast majority of the stockless type.

Stockless Anchor Stowage

Most vessels had their hawse pipes carefully angled to afford easy access for the anchor shank. In some a stop was fitted for the anchor bills to bear against. Reinforcement round the hawse pipe was common, as was a wedge-shaped section weld-

The Philadelphia Engineering Co's 'Peco' stockless, sanctioned on 17 March 1921. (Lloyd's Register of Shipping)

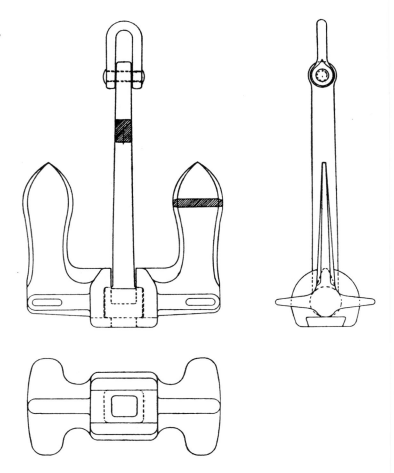

ed to the hull below the hawse pipe for easier stowage. Stockless anchors were fitted with a large 'D' shackle at the top of the shank to attach them to the plain link at the end of the anchor cable, a 'D' joining shackle being used for this.

To put these developments in perspective, in 1815 the largest anchors used in HM Ships weighed 4½ tons, but their length was almost the same as the stockless anchor of RMS *Queen Mary* of the twentieth century; weights differed, however, the latter's anchors weighing 16 tons.

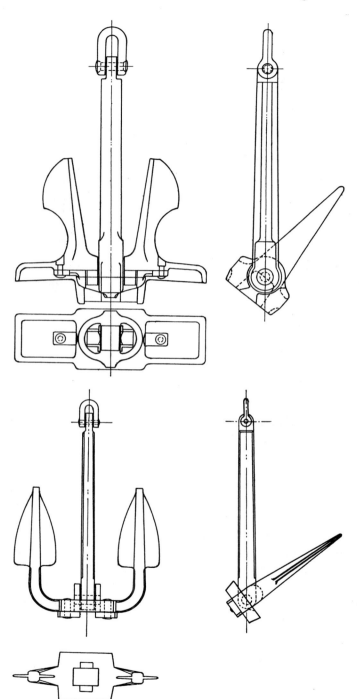

The 'Gruson-Hein'
stockless, by W Hein of
Bremen, sanctioned 11
August 1927. (Lloyd's
Register of Shipping)

The 'Rynvaart Nieuw
Model', by Koninklijke
Nederlandsche
Grofsmederij of Leiden,
sanctioned 25 July
1939. (Lloyd's
Register of Shipping)

Stowage of the modern stockless anchors at the hawse pipes of the bulk carrier Spey Bridge. (Author)

High holding power anchors

At the end of the nineteenth century tests on commercial stockless anchors showed roughly the same holding power for all–about six times their own weight. It was obviously time for a considerable improvement in holding power.

The designation High Holding Power is given to an anchor that is shown in full scale trials in three types of ground, soft mud or silt, sand or gravel, and hard clay or similar compact soil, to be at least twice as efficient as a standard stockless type of anchor of the same weight.

The increasing size of vessels by the twentieth century demanded the above, specially for the VLCC (very large crude [oil] carriers). Their huge draught meant lying offshore at a considerable distance, so security of mooring was essential. They usually carried two bower anchors and a spare, which might weigh as much as 30 tons each. The chain cables for each used 130 tons of steel; likely costs were £20,000 to £30,000 for each anchor.

The Admiralty began extensive trials from 1943 onwards starting with an Admiralty Stockless Anchor and similar commercial anchors in general use. All had short flukes, large crowns and heavy shanks. The tests included dragging the anchors 50 feet, when they rotated 180 degrees and emerged from the sea bed with flukes inclined upwards. Further trials in 1950 were carried out on the AC10 (Admiralty Cast) apparently very successfully, but on a very hard sea bed the anchor dragged till the flukes caught on an obstruction, when it stood on the points, causing the anchor to 'walk' until it reached softer ground affording it a grip.

Modifications and further tests followed; the AC11 and AC12 were produced, the latter a High Holding Power anchor. It was established that fluke area, not the weight, was the most important factor for most sea bed conditions, and confirmed that a proper scope of chain was critical if the anchor was to bed itself properly. The AC14 was the result of Admiralty trials during the Second World War. It was one of the first large High Holding Power anchors, although not approved as such by Lloyd's Register until 1964. The original design had hollow flukes, but the manufacturing costs of casting and fabrication were greater than anticipated, so a solid-fluke design, heavier and less efficient in terms of the ratio of holding power to weight, was adapted for use in the Royal and other navies. The AC14 was popular in the 1950s to 1960s, and about 2½-3 times as efficient as the early Admiralty Standard Stockless Anchor.

A number of designs, for commercial use also, were so successful that after 1966 Lloyd's Register allowed a 25 per cent reduction in weight for designs approved as High Holding anchors. Trials of some of the latter showed them to be at least twice as efficient as the standard stockless anchor of the same weight, some proving four times better.

It was noted that an anchor must withstand being dropped on solid rock, and the actual mass of it was critical on very poor holding ground. For some types of soft ground, holding power improved if the fluke angle was increased to around 45-50 degrees. In good holding ground, angles of 30-32 degrees were commonly used. Care of fluke tips was all-important.

Other High Holding Power anchors were approved in the next few years, including, unexpectedly, the CQR. The list also

Right:
The (Admiralty Cast) AC14. (From the Admiralty *Manual of Seamanship*)

Far right:
The Danforth Anchor. As a High Holding Power anchor Lloyd's and Germanische Lloyd allow a 25 per cent weight reduction over the specified equipment weight for conventional forms; Bureau Veritas and American Bureau allow 20 per cent.
(From the Admiralty *Manual of Seamanship*)

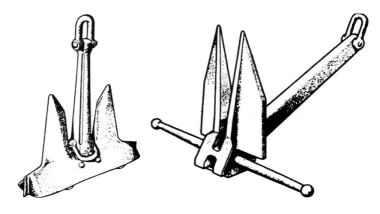

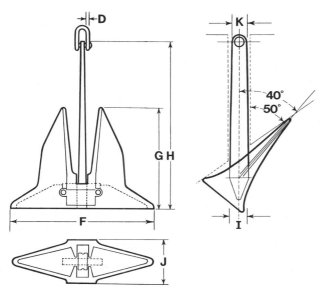

The Stokes Bower Stockless Anchor. The design uses wing-like extensions of the flukes instead of a stock at the crown; it is manufactured in sizes up to 40,000 pounds and is allowed a 25 per cent weight reduction by classification societies. (Author)

A US Navy Lightweight type of about 1944; this Canadian example weighs 2000 pounds. (National Defence Photo, by RCN)

Lightweight Anchors fitted to the semi-submersible oil rig Bideford Dolphin. *The anchors are stowed on outriggers, with the cables led to windlasses on the upper platform.* (AS Bergens Mekaniske Verksteder, Bergen)

includes the designs of Stokes, Byers, Bruce and Stevin. All share a large fluke area, and except the CQR, have stabilising fins to avoid rolling over. The Stevin, with concave flukes, hollow like the first AC14, was developed with very strong construction for offshore and dredging work, but also approved as a ship's anchor.

The Danforth Anchor of 1939 and the United States Navy Lightweight Anchor were both patented in the 1940s, both relying on stocks for stability. These are placed at the heads of the anchors in the same plane as the flukes, thus easing problems of handling. The Danforth flukes are sharply pointed, the anchor being specially efficient in a hard sea bed. The US Navy

Lightweight Anchor, developed in the Second World War as a High Holding anchor, was fitted in naval ships from 1944 onwards. It was often supplied to landing craft as a stern anchor for hauling off beaches. In this case it was stowed in a special vertical stowage on the V-shaped transom stern of the craft.

An anti-tripping stock fitted at the anchor head enables it to be used as a bower anchor while retaining the capability of hawse pipe stowage. In the 1970s it was used extensively for mooring semi-submersible oil platforms. Both these anchors were approved as High Holding Power anchors by Lloyd's Register of Shipping, the Danforth in 1964 and the US Lightweight in 1966.

The Submarine Anchors AC16 and AC17

An Admiralty Cast anchor not yet considered is the AC16. This was designed specifically for submarines, after the earlier practice of arrangements similar to surface ships had to be discontinued. The introduction of high-speed heavy nuclear-powered submarines demanded an anchor which, when stowed, is flush with the hull and completely closes the hull opening. For obvious reasons it must be lowered and raised by remote control.

The Admiralty Cast AC16A was the prototype, designed for and carried in HMS *Dreadnought*, the Royal Navy's first nuclear submarine. Designed for stowage flush with the hull it was stowed vertically in the underside of the boat, and its closure checked by remote control. Its curved crown maintained the streamlining of the vessel.

The AC17 followed, also from the Admiralty Experimental Works. In simple terms its operation is as follows: when the anchor cable is drawn up into the hawse pipe a spigot engages in a cam or spiral groove which turns the anchor into the fore and aft line so that it enters the hawse pipe correctly. A cut-out switch stops the cable holder when the anchor is home and stowed. This anchor, a High Holding Power model, is also considered suitable for vessels with a bulbous bow such as a VLCC

The AC16A itself may be seen on the anchor park of the National Maritime Museum. Both anchor and this class of submarine have been replaced by more modern designs; it is understood that two anchors are now carried, but details of these are naturally not available to the public.

1.

2.

3.

4.

Less common High Holding Power types. From top:
1. Union Leichtgewichts Anker, German manufacture, 500 to 3500kg weight.
2. Pool (fabricated head), Dutch manufacture, 12,000 to 16,000kg weight.
3. Stevin Mark II, Dutch manufacture, 500 to 15,000kg weight.
4. Table Anchor, used for dredging and offshore work. (Author)

Above: *The AC16A
Anchor from the first
British nuclear
submarine, HMS/M*
Dreadnought.
(Author)

Below: *The developed
Admiralty submarine
anchor, AC17.* (From
the Admiralty *Manual
of Seamanship*)

Below: *The bottom-
stowage arrangements
of the AC17*

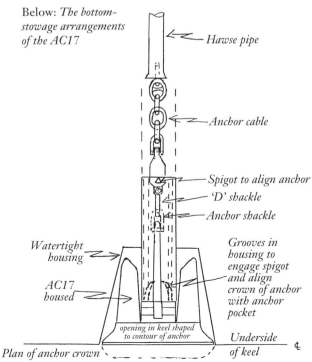

Hawse pipe

Anchor cable

Spigot to align anchor

'D' shackle

Anchor shackle

Grooves in
housing to
engage spigot
and align
crown of anchor
with anchor
pocket

Watertight
housing

AC17
housed

*opening in keel shaped
to contour of anchor*

Underside
of keel

Plan of anchor crown

Single-fluke and mooring anchors | 14

Mooring anchors

In a paper read to the Institution of Naval Architects in March 1950 Mr H L Dove defined very clearly the function of the mooring anchor compared with that carried constantly in a sea-going vessel.

> This anchor is employed in permanent moorings to supply a firm hold on the sea bed for the attachment of a vertical pendant chain leading to a buoy. This chain passes through the buoy and is attached to the buoy shackle, to which the ship secures its own mooring chain or wire. This type of anchor is lowered to a position just above the sea bed, and dropped into the sea bed. The lowering and dropping are controlled, and it is therefore possible to ensure that the anchor will always enter the sea bed in a required attitude. It therefore has a single fixed fluke. Stabilization is added by means of a fixed stock, which prevents the anchor rolling out of its bed.

In this paper he did not, however, consider another function of the single fluke-anchor – to anchor a floating stage alongside a dockyard wall in permanent moorings. On a falling tide, here a ship risked sitting on the upturned fluke of a normal stocked anchor.

The accompanying drawing shows the use of heavy ground

Mooring to a buoy.
(Author)

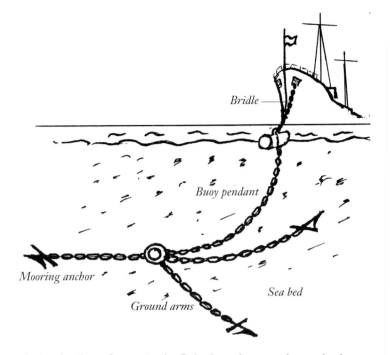

chains leading from single-fluked anchors and attached to a central ring which lies on the harbour bottom. A single length of cable known as the buoy pendant is attached to this ring. The upper end of this passes through, and is supported by, a mooring buoy. To the upper end of the buoy pendant is

The National Maritime Museum's single-fluke anchor. (National Maritime Museum)

attached the large buoy shackle, and to this (usually referred to as the buoy ring), the ship secures the end of her anchor cable; a swivel is fitted to the buoy pendant to prevent it becoming twisted as the ship swings with wind or tide. The part of the cable between ship and buoy is termed the bridle. Although the ship is said to be moored to the buoy, it is in fact moored to the permanent chain mooring.

The National Maritime Museum owns a single-fluke anchor, displayed on the anchor park. This is fitted with a replica wooden stock, the original being 20 feet across, and the shank 13 feet long. Its weight is about 1 ton, and holding power weight x 2. It is believed to have been used to haul vessels off the Deptford Dockyard after repairs or refit.

Interestingly, enquiries are regularly received at the Museum concerning Admiralty-type anchors found with one arm twisted round the shank. This was done by heating the arm to a very high temperature, and forcing it round the shank to reproduce the mooring anchor described above, and for the same purpose. Such finds are almost invariably made in harbours; for example, one of them was found in the harbour of Zanzibar.

Admiralty Mooring Anchors

The earliest known drawing of an Admiralty mooring block or anchor is dated 11 October 1809 and signed by Samuel Hemmans, the Master Attendant at Chatham Dockyard. Part of his responsibility involved the care of the numerous ships

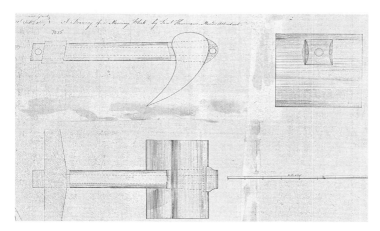

The original draught of Hemmans Anchor, 1809. (National Maritime Museum DR7635)

The 'Tombstone' – the Admiralty Mooring Anchor Mark I; this example is at Culross, Scotland. (Author)

laid up in Ordinary (what would now be called Reserve) in the River Medway, so he had a real interest in improved mooring arrangements. The anchor takes the form of a heavy fixed 'claw' or fluke, the shank being 10 feet long, all presumably fabricated of iron. In principle it is not significantly different from later Admiralty designs like the Mark I or the recent AM7 described below.

Although the Admiralty also employed the Mushroom-type anchor, as well as blocks for permanent moorings, there was a series of large single-fluke anchors specially designed for the purpose. Because they are not usually dropped or embedded by dragging, they need only one fluke, but they have a stock to prevent the anchor rolling out of its bed. The Admiralty Mooring Anchor Mark I of about 1900 was very substantial, and known as the Tombstone. Preserved examples survive at both Gibraltar and Malta, but the one illustrated commemorates the construction in 1907-27 of the Rosyth Naval Base where it was used; it was presented to Culross by the Naval Base Commander in June 1993.

A developed version of this was the AM7, which had a one-piece fluke and shank, the latter curved back at a more acute

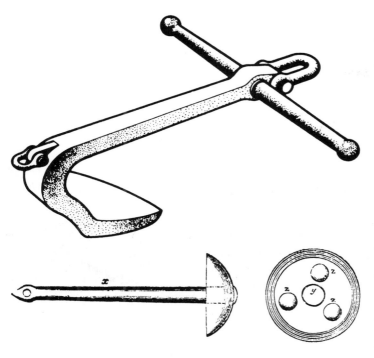

Left: *Mushroom Anchor.* (From George Cotsell's *A Treatise on Ships' Anchors,* 1856)

Below: *A model of the Parachute Anchor.* (National Maritime Museum)

angle on itself than in the Mark I; as well as the shackle at the end of the shank, there was a lifting eye for another shackle cast on the outside of the curve at the 'crown'.

The Mushroom or Parachute Anchor

Introduced and patented about 1840, no authority has mentioned this anchor with anything like enthusiasm. It consisted of a hemispherical crown, into which was inserted a shank with a collar to be clenched on the outer side. Openings, usually three, were pierced in the crown so that mud or sand that came up as the anchor was raised, could fall away through these. It seems to have been most effective on a mud or sand sea bed, but as George Cotsell wrote in his *Treatise on Ships' Anchors,* 'Its holding power could scarcely equal the ordinary anchor, whilst the trouble of forging the crown was immense and in heavy anchors, beyond all calculation. The name of the inventor is not known to me . . .'. Hardly surprising, as he concludes crushingly, 'Neither nautically nor mechanically were its advantages such as to recommend it. As an anchor it falls short of the essentials necessary to success.'

However, ignoring Cotsell, the crews of some early submarines were brave enough to carry them, and the heaviest amongst them were used to secure the Boom Defence at Portsmouth during the Second World War. Note that the Parachute version of this type has four points marked on its circumference between which the plain Mushroom design is cut away in four segments.

Mooring Screws

Designed and patented in 1833 by Alexander Mitchell, these consisted of a single turn of a cast-iron screw of large diameter and small pitch, provided on its lower surface with a gimlet point. In one of his types the screw was fitted with a shank by which it could be rotated, thus forcing its way into the ground. The top of this shank was provided with a shackle and swivel for receiving the mooring chain. In another type the screw had a short stem, over which was fitted the socket used in sinking it, but which was afterwards removed, the mooring chain and buoy being then attached to the short chain secured to the screw. The serrated edge shown on these screws was a later improvement which was found to facilitate rotation and entrance in stony ground. One of these mooring screws, 4 feet

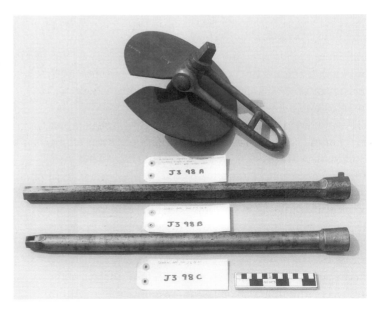

Models of Mitchell's Mooring Screws. (National Maritime Museum C8839/19)

in diameter, weighs 11.5 hundredweight and is used with a 1.5-inch cable. [From the 1911 Catalogue of the Naval and Marine Engineering Collection then held in the Science Museum]

These anchors were never employed as part of a sea-going ship's equipment, but were generally used for hulks. A double-screw mooring might be used in a barge 'road' off the navigational channel, in the care of a watchman. Fifty years ago the barge traffic on the Thames was so extensive that public barge 'roads' were available for nearly 9000 barges to lie up when not being navigated. [*PLA Monthly*, April 1927]

A specially designed screw lighter was necessary to screw these anchors in position. Navigational buoys may also use the screw or the clump anchor type; in addition, screw anchors have also been employed in connection with the bases of pile lighthouses.

Mooring Clump or Block Anchors

These are large blocks of cast iron or cast steel, primarily used to secure buoys for navigational marks, or when required, boom defences. They are, as illustrated, plain blocks of various forms with a securing shackle at the top, or lifting and mooring eyes. An early Admiralty type proposed by James Park, Master Attendant at Portsmouth Dockyard, was adopted in September 1815.

One type, not surprisingly, was designed by the ubiquitous Lt William Rodger in 1819, known as his Makeshift Mooring Anchor, and another by him in 1851. Both these were wedge-shaped, deeper at the base than at the front. This type does not dig deep into the sea bed, but pushes a

Top: *A model of Park's 1815 design of mooring block.* (National Maritime Museum C8838/10a)

Middle: *A model of Rodger's Makeshift Mooring Anchor.* (National Maritime Museum C8838/11a)

Bottom: *A model of Rodger's 1851 design of mooring block.* (National Maritime Museum C8838/14a)

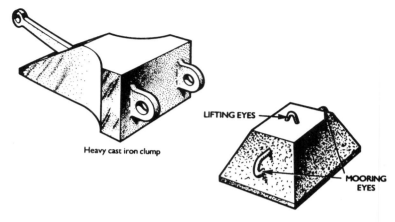

Admiralty heavy cast iron (left) and concrete clumps. (From the Admiralty *Manual of Seamanship*)

mound of sand in front of it when dragged. As this is scoured away the process is repeated.

In 1901 Mr C G Lenox patented his design of this type, a development of the earlier mooring clump previously adopted by the Admiralty. First tried in the River Orwell on hard smooth ground, results were very good on such an unfavourable sea bed.

The holding power of these wedge-shaped anchors was found to be at least three times that of some other forms. They were made in various sizes from 1 to 12 tons weight.

Concrete Mooring Clumps, also used, were eventually damaged by sea water, losing 40 per cent of their effectiveness. They were appropriate for navigational marks, and 6th class moorings. Cast iron sinkers lose 14 per cent effectiveness in sea water, but are effective for light buoy moorings and navigational buoys. These usually have a lifting eye on the top.

The Rarotonga Anchor

In the *Pacific Islands Monthly* of December 1968, Robert Langdon wrote an account of a curious-looking anchor believed to be a relic of a shipwreck on a reef at Ngatanglia, on the eastern side of Rarotonga in the Cook Islands. Four survivors of the wreck got ashore, runs the tale, and after kindly treatment by local people, the captain of the wrecked ship, named *Kora*, gave a sword which, together with the curious anchor, was in the possession of Mr Charlie Cowan. Mr Cowan, half-Scots, half-Rarotongan and then aged 82, told the reporter the wrecked ship's main anchor lay in the Ngatanglia lagoon, where a ship built there in 1891 used it as a mooring anchor. That anchor appears to have been lost, unlike the one described here which was found on the beach where *Kora* was wrecked. The survivors then vanished one night in a stolen canoe.

The significant part of this account is the strong resemblance of this anchor – a drawing as well as a photograph accompanied the story – to the AM7 mooring anchor described earlier in this chapter. Its size is

The fluke and eye of the Rarotongan anchor, Cook Islands. (Van Eijk & Meers)

smaller but the basic design and form are the same – even a hole at the back of the anchor's curve appears to be in the same position as the lifting eye and shackle on the curve of the AM 7. Mr Cowan, a keen student of Rarotongan history, stated that originally a length of chain had been attached to the 'loop' of the anchor. It is tempting to imagine that *Kora* – nothing else appears known of her – had found her way finally from England carrying a possible predecessor of an Admiralty type anchor.

Innovative types

It should be understood that by terming these anchors 'innovative' it is meant only that they were indeed so when the designs first appeared. The purpose of this book is to describe in historic sequence the evolution of anchor design from stone anchor to stockless, and even as it is written, some of the innovative anchors described will have been succeeded by a more advanced version of the old, or by one totally new in concept. However, whatever the pattern, their purpose will remain the same – to hold a vessel securely in the haven it seeks.

The Seastaple

Associated with the sunshine on Pacific beaches, Mr Cowan's Rarotongan discovery may seem more enticing than the embedment anchor developed by the US Army Material Command's Engineering Research and Development Laboratories, but the latter is even more exotic. This anchor was designed for the petroleum industry's offshore operations where the mooring wire must be held in a vertical position. It was given the name Seastaple to suggest its action.

Security of mooring was essential to the North Sea drilling platforms. While earlier platforms had been built to drill in depths up to 600 feet, in the mid-1970s depths up to 1200 feet could be reached. The Seastaple was one heavy High Holding Power anchor designed for this use. Produced in two sizes, the Mk 50 had an anchor weight of 535 pounds and overall length of 8 feet 9 inches, and holding power of 22 tons; the larger, Mk 300, weighed 1300 pounds, its length was 12 feet 9 inches and holding power 134 tons.

In operation the anchor assembly is 'fired' vertically into the sea bed to a depth of 20-30 feet. The vibrating driving head, fluidising the bottom material round the anchor, drives the fluke assembly into the ground. The 'gun' with the recoil assembly moves upwards a few feet and is recovered for re-use by a separate retrieving line. The anchor once embedded will develop its rated holding power and will not drag. Its hawser is of flat, multi-strand assembly with a swagged fitting at each end. When the anchor is fixed the hawser is progressively stripped from the assembly. It is covered with a coat of tough plastic to protect the metal interior against corrosion and bottom abrasion.

The Bruce Anchor

The Bruce Anchor; this is the smallest, 2kg, size. (The Bruce Anchor Co, Edinburgh)

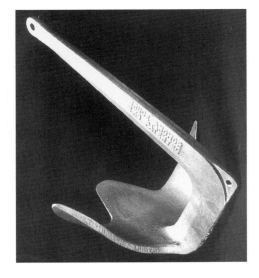

Developed by the company of the same name, this is considered one of the best modern anchors, for both mooring and sea-going use. Of one-piece construction it resembles a single-fluke mooring anchor without a stock, and with wide curved extensions on each side of the fluke. These 'self-orienting' extensions force it to an upward attitude as it engages the sea bed; the makers consider it will bury with the cable at an angle of up to 30 degrees at the anchor shackle, compared with a maximum of 10 to 15 degrees for other anchors. The three points of the fluke enable it to grip on rocky sea beds.

It is made in sizes from 2kg to 50kg, suitable for vessels up to 28 metres overall. While there are no parts to clog or jam, it has been suggested that in a sea bed of mud and stone, a ball of this forming in the anchor palm might reduce efficiency.

The Doris Mud Anchor

The need for an anchor capable of holding in a soft sea bed became obvious when semi-submersible drilling rigs, drilling ships and derrick barges needed secure mooring. The Paris-based anchor designers and manufacturers, C G Doris, produced their mud anchor, which basically acted like a shovel to bury itself securely.

The anchor consists of a large concave plate or shovel attached to two arms with distances-pieces between them. The 'shovel' is concave, enabling the anchor to sink in when under the pull of its cable. The makers term this the chassis, which has two inclined screens ensuring rigidity and completing the burying action of the anchor. 'In a mud cohesion of 50 to 100 grammes per centimetre the theoretical holding power is from 20 to 360 tons, according to the size of anchor chosen.'

Basically it is a large anchor varying from a weight of 1.5 tonnes to 45 tonnes. The length, width and height of the smallest is 3 metres, 2.8 metres, and 1 metre respectively, and its holding power claimed in tonnes is 20. These dimensions rise proportionately. It is also of simple but effective construction: a chain bridle at the end of the chassis arms meets at a junction plate shackled to the anchor cable. The locating and handling devices are of three main parts: a

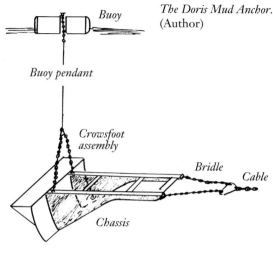

The Doris Mud Anchor. (Author)

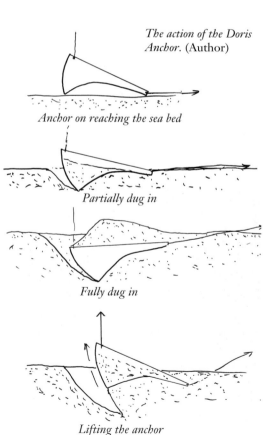

The action of the Doris Anchor. (Author)

Anchor on reaching the sea bed

Partially dug in

Fully dug in

Lifting the anchor

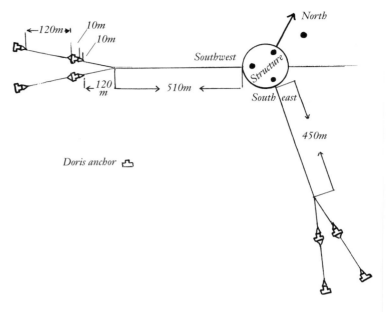

The layout of Doris action (Author)

'crowfoot' assembly attached to the anchor, a buoy rope and a marker buoy.

The CQR Anchor

This anchor was designed and developed by Professor Sir Geoffrey Ingram Taylor, FRS. It was patented by a small private company, with Mr George McKerrow as a director, together with Sir Geoffrey and Sir William Farren. A shorter name than that originally proposed was felt desirable to catch the eye, and Mr McKerrow, in the privacy of his bath, dreamt up the initials CQR, which have no other significance. It was patented in 1933 as an anchor for flying boats, where high holding power and lightness were essential.

It became popular on yachts, and more than popular during the Second World War when 60,000 anchors of varying sizes were ordered by the Admiralty and the Fairmile company amongst others, at least 45,000 being delivered. Many of the anchors delivered were of the 45-pound and 60-pound types. Combined Operations ordered non-magnetic versions for their wartime raids, and landing craft used them as stern anchors. Another version was used in association with the Mulberry Harbour. After the end of the war, the patent was sold to the North British Welding Company.

The following is taken from McKerrow's account of the anchor's beginnings:

> The many cases of flying boats dragging their anchor in the poor holding ground of estuaries, preferred as they offered room to anchor, worried Sir Geoffrey, then member of the Aeronautics Advisory Committee. The CQR came to him in a flash.

McKerrow saw first the prototype made by Sir Geoffrey, weighing 1 or 2 pounds. The latter demonstrated how the anchor's sharp point dug itself in, needing a sharp pull to move it. The then Mr Farren got the design 'frozen'. McKerrow continued:

> I got a number of anchors made, kept them in a pit in my garage, and sold then in ones and twos. We wanted a test at sea, so in 1934 chartered a yacht in Unst, most northerly of the Shetland Islands, and replaced the yacht's own 130-pound anchor with a CQR of 50 pounds which proved adequate.

Professor Sir Geoffrey Ingram Taylor and Charles H Stocks, senior Lloyd's surveyor, testing the prototype CQR Anchor in London's West India Dock. This 3 hundredweight model resisted a pull of 10 tons and did not drag, compared with a standard stockless of 5 hundredweight which registered only ³/₄ ton, although a standard Admiralty pattern did rather better than the latter. (Express Photos)

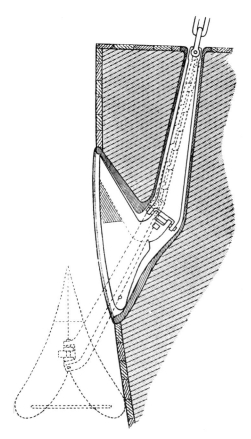

How the CQR is housed.
(From *The Motor Boat*,
4 December 1936)

They tried the Air Ministry who refused the normal model, but willingly paid 'a fantastic price, accepted without a murmur, for a model machined all over'. They tried the Merchant Marine, 'but came up against legislation laying down certain weights, and showed no interest in efficiency.' The War Office was equally uninterested: 'An elderly colonel had apparently been nearly drowned in an obscure river somewhere in the foothills of the Himalayas through the fluke of an anchor penetrating the pontoon in which he had embarked. He disliked pointed anchors, and the CQR had a point . . . .'

As recorded earlier, the outbreak of the Second World War changed all that, and orders from the Services came flooding in; Mountbatten, having seen tests, was very favourably impressed. The finest accolade came from a US officer inspecting landing craft under construction in Australia for Pacific operations. He described the landing craft as 'the world's worst crate that ever went to sea, saved by the world's best anchor.' The only sad point was that it could not be claimed as invented in the States.

McKerrow again: 'When the question of easy stowage for the CQR arose this was solved by the production of a short shank variation which could be pulled into a suitably designed hawse pipe so as to lie flush with the side of the boat.' Its advantages were reported in *The Motor Boat* of December 1936: 'Roughly speaking, it is claimed that the CQR anchor of a given weight holds two or three times as well as a stocked anchor, which in its turn, is always much better than a stockless anchor, sometimes to the extent of two or three times.'

In this survey of anchor history the CQR is the only one that has been handled frequently by the author. Two, one large, one small, were carried in a small yacht and fully justified the enthusiasm of the designers. The misfortune of tripping over the larger one, lashed on the foredeck in place of its smaller replica, while lowering the jib, and promptly falling into the unsavoury waters of Haslar Creek, was in no way detrimental to the anchor's excellent reputation. Nor was the loss of another in a lake in Italy, when the flying boat carrying it made a forced landing: the radio operator, in charge of anchoring it threw the CQR out correctly, but had failed to secure its cable to the flying boat!

The CQR set a trend for plough anchors, of which there are now several varieties, like the Delta, intended for the burgeoning modern yacht market. The CQR was drop-forged, as opposed to cast, which the manufacturers always claimed led to far greater strength, but modern anchors – especially lightweight models for small craft – are often made of alloys or aluminium.

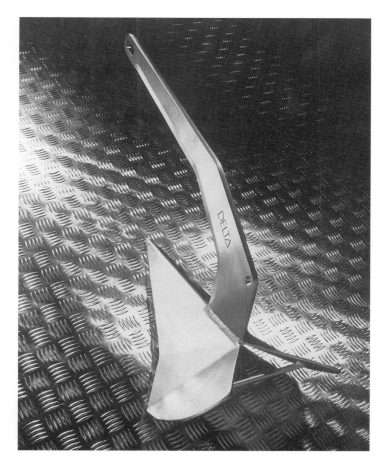

The modern Delta Anchor. (Simpson Lawrence Ltd)

Appendix:
Testing anchors
and cables

The following is one of the earliest known accounts of a proposal for testing of anchors. Its discovery was due to the researches of Commander W E May, then of the National Maritime Museum. It is taken from a collection of Portsmouth Dockyard Officers' reports to the Commissioner (who represented the Navy Board) from 6 January 1703/4 to 4 June 1709, the originals being in the care of the Museum. The anchor shown was probably intended to represent the Old Admiralty Longshank of the period, although the curving arms are untypical.

Honoured Sir,

Portsmouth Dockyard 8 January 1704

According to your honoured directions I have prepared the enclosed sketch of the lever or engine I propose for trying of anchors. At the end of which steelyard or lever there is a due proportion of weight to be put according to the strength of each cable by Establishment allowed to anchors of the several weights, which by experiment being nearly [*ie* closely] calculated and by me duly considered, I hope there will be an effectual way of proving anchors of all weights: which engine or levers may be made of old timber and the charge thereof will not amount to above £25 or £30, I am

Honoured Sir
Your most Humble and Obedient Servant
JR.

To Commissioner Gifford

The Ground Plan

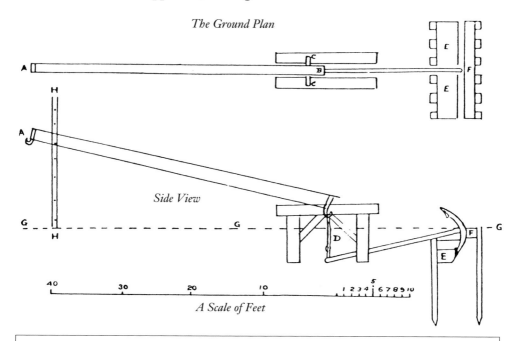

Side View

A Scale of Feet

A:B	The beam or steelyard		at E & F (the palm and crown) by timber work in the ground, it will be a natural strain both to fluke and shank.
A	The end where the weight is to be hung		
C	The centre [fulcrum] where the beam turns	G:G:G	Represents the surface of the ground
D	The hook or chain that takes the ring of the anchor; which anchor being confined	H:H	Two upright pieces between which the end of the beam rises and falls

In Chapter 10 the increasing need for proving chain cables and chains has been noted. Samuel Brown was one of the first to design a Proving Machine, and various Proving Houses, including one controlled by Trinity House, issued certificates covering chain cables and anchors. In 1833 Proving Machines were first made and used in Government Dockyards at Woolwich and Plymouth.

An early anchor testing rig from Portsmouth Dockyard, dated 8 January 1704 and signed 'JR'. (National Maritime Museum, Portsmouth Dockyard records)

Writing as late as 1885, Thomas Traill felt compelled to criticise unscrupulous manufacturers who took advantage of the increasing demand for chain cables, their flawed products often resulting in tragedy. However, it had been obvious much earlier that as the size of cables increased Government legislation would be essential to control their quality.

In 1864 the first Act covering the supply of cables and

anchors to British merchant vessels was passed, regulating their proving and sale. This was followed by an Amendment Act in 1871, suspended, however, in 1872 by a brief Act until January 1873. In 1874 a further Act was passed providing for the correct certification of anchors and cables to be in a condition of seaworthiness. All anchors weighing 168 pounds and upwards were to be tested prior to sale.

In 1876 the Board of Trade instructed their Surveyors that all vessels which came under survey for a passenger certificate should show proof that all anchors over 168 pounds in weight had been duly tested in accordance with the provisions of the Chain Cables and Anchors Acts of 1864 to 1874. If proof was not forthcoming, it would be the shipowner's responsibility to have the items concerned re-tested and the necessary certificates obtained. This not only involved newly constructed ships; those already afloat had to comply with the requirements of this law as well.

Commercial Classification Rules

Under the various Acts since 1864, it has been a legal requirement to test all anchors of above 168 pounds weight designed for merchant ships, and mark them as shown in the drawing. Up to metrification, anchor weights were expressed in hundredweights (cwt), quarters (qrs) and pounds (lbs). The size of anchors carried depended on the equipment number in the relevant classification society rules, but foreign-going ships usually carried two bowers and a spare, and sometimes also a stern or stream anchor. The head of the anchor had to constitute 60 per cent of the total weight of a stockless anchor, and the angle between the shank and the arms was from 30 to 40 degrees, usually nearer the latter.

Until the twentieth century most anchors were made of forged wrought iron, but forged ingot steel or cast steel has been used since. The former were heated after manufacture to restore their molecular structure, and then subjected to tensile and cold-bend tests. Cast anchors were annealed by heating them to 850-950 degrees Centigrade, and allowing them to cool at a uniform rate, after which they were given a drop test (castings over 15 hundredweight were dropped from a height of 12 feet on to a steel slab). The anchor was then raised off the ground and struck with a 7-pound hammer, when it was

Left fluke	Shank	Right fluke

Mark of
assigning
authority (eg Lloyd's)
Weight of head
Surveyor's initials
No of drop test certificate
Date of drop test

Same marks as right fluke
Total weight of anchor (near shackle)

Proving house
identification mark
No of test certificate
No of tensile test machine
Year of licence of machine
Applied proof strain
Government mark

expected to give a clear ring; if it did not, a flaw was assumed, and the anchor was rejected.

The various subsequent Acts require a chapter at least to themselves, and to follow their details is probably beyond the interest of the average reader. 'The Anchor and Chain Cable Rules' laid down in 1970 involve not only definition of the tests, but also of each component of chain or anchor, definition of the Certifying Authority, of each term used, of the installation of the testing premises and the design and construction of the testing machines and their dates of inspection. Thanks, however, to the kindness of Mr M Cobbold, in 1980 Superintendent of the Marine Services School and Salvage Depot at HM Naval Base, Rosyth, a straightforward account of the naval testing process now follows.

Royal Navy Testing Practice

Angle of flukes – (stockless anchors)

1. The anchor is laid flat on a smooth steel slab not less than 76mm (3 inches) thickness.
2. The flukes are then raised to the full designed angle to which they open and then gently pushed back until they fall.
3. Turn anchor over and repeat operation. Check maximum angle of throw conforms to designed angle on both sides.

Drop test

1. Each anchor or portion of anchor whose weight is 0.76 tonnes (15 hundredweight) or less shall be raised to a height of 4.6m (15 feet) and then dropped on a steel slab well laid out on solid concrete of equivalent foundation.

2. Anchors or portions of anchors whose weight exceeds 0.76 tonnes (15 hundredweight) shall be raised to a height of 3.6m (12 feet).

3. Atmospheric temperature when drop tests are carried out shall not be below 10 degrees Centigrade.

Hammer test

After completion of the drop test, each cast steel anchor or part of an anchor is slung freely and subjected to such hammering test necessary to prove the soundness of the casting and freedom from flaws.

Proof test

Anchor is then tested to proof load specified for that anchor.

FOR MANUFACTURERS

Marking of anchors

Every anchor and stock that has passed the stipulated proof test shall be distinctly marked in a conspicuous place with the letters

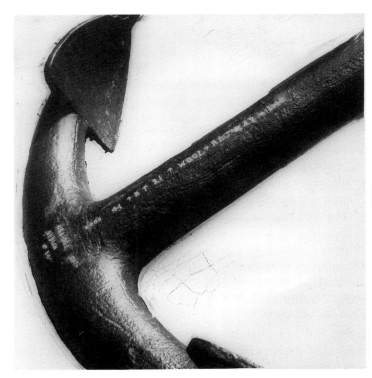

Markings on an Admiralty anchor: on the shank is the number (6089), the weight (41 - 2 - 21, in hundredweight - quarters - pounds), the Dockyard (Woolwich) and date received (7 May 1848). (Author)

MOD [Ministry of Defence] indicating the certifying authority.

Additionally, each anchor shall be stamped by the manufacturers with the weight and the words FORGED STEEL or CAST STEEL as appropriate and the initials of the certifying officer. In the case of portions of anchors made of cast steel, the words CAST STEEL and the name or trademark of the maker shall also be cast or stamped in. The statutory marking shall not be stamped until the proof load has been applied.

Special regulations also exist for marking anchors after examination and repair. Before reissue they are to be marked on the shank as follows: examined, mark with letter E, repaired with letter R, and proof tested with letter T. These are to be followed by the initial letter of the Naval Base where either or all of these requirements were carried out; then the year they were carried out; test load applied if applicable. Typical marking may then appear as follows: ER T56.8 Tonne D 1974. These marks show that the anchor was examined, repaired and proof tested to a proof load of 56.8 tonnes at Devonport in 1974.

Sadly this very comprehensive series of tests is no longer at Rosyth Naval Base, which closed, it is understood, in 1998.

American Bureau of Shipping Marks

The requirements for US mercantile anchors were similar in principle to their British equivalents, but the rules were as follows.

Stocked anchors

These were made of forged wrought iron, forged open-hearth ingot steel, or cast steel; the stock had to be a quarter the weight of the anchor. No vessel could be classed with the letter (E) unless the anchor had been tested and the weights were in the required ratio to the tonnage of the vessel.

Stockless anchors

The weight of the head had to be not less than three-fifths of the total weight of the anchor. One side of the anchor was reserved for the marks shown in the drawing, and the other side solely for the maker's name or trademark. If the design of the anchor did not allow the standard positioning of the marks shown, a suitable boss had to be cast on each arm on which the marks were stamped.

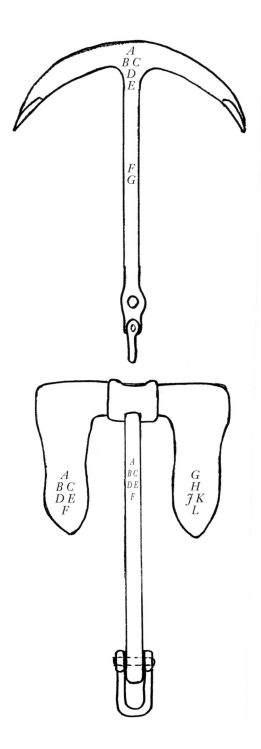

Stocked anchor markings required by the American Bureau of Shipping. (Author)

A. The number of the certificate
B. The initials of the Surveyor who witnessed the test
C. Month and year of test
D. Proof test applied, in pounds
E. Sign that the test machine is recognised by the American Bureau of Shipping
F. The weight of the anchor, excluding the stock, in pounds
G. The weight of the stock, in pounds

Stockless anchor markings required by the American Bureau of Shipping. (Author)

A. The number of the proof certificate
B. The initials of the Surveyor who witnessed the proof test
C. Month and year of proof test
D. Proof test applied, in pounds
E. Sign that the test machine is recognised by the American Bureau of Shipping
F. The weight of the anchor, in pounds
G. Sign that the anchor head has been tested by a surveyor to the Bureau
H. The weight of the anchor head, in pounds
J. The initials of the Surveyor who witnessed the drop test
K. The number of drop test certificate
L. Month and year of drop test

Bibliography

William Burney, *Marine Dictionary*, London 1815

Pieter le Comte, *Praktikale Zeevaartkunde*, Amsterdam 1842

George Cotsell, *A Treatise on Ships' Anchors*, London 1856

William Falconer, *Universal Dictionary of the Marine*, London 1769

John Fincham, *An Introductory Outline to the Practice of Shipbuilding*, London 1825

Ian Friel, *The Good Ship: Ships, Shipbuilding and Technology in England 1200-1520*, London 1995

Richard Haklyut, *The Principal Navigations, Voyages, Traffiques and discoveries of the English Nation*, London 1589

International Journal of Nautical Archaeology (quarterly, 1972-)

Lloyd's Register of Shipping, *Anchors – Approved Designs*, London 1945

Sir Henry Mainwaring, *Seaman's Dictionary*, London 1622

N J McDermaid, *Shipyard Practice*, London 1917.

Dr F Moll, 'The history of the anchor', *The Mariner's Mirror* XIII (1927)

K Nicholau & H W Catling, 'Composite anchors in Late Bronze Age Cyprus', *Antiquity* 42, pp225-9.

Richard Pering, *A Treatise on the Anchor*, Plymouth 1819

M W Prynne, 'Henry V's *Grace Dieu*', *The Mariner's Mirror* 54 (1968)

William Rodger, *Explanatory Observations*, London 1852

John Smith, *A Sea Grammar*, London 1627

Carl V Sølver, *Om Ankre*, Copenhagen 1945

David Steel, *Elements & Practice of Rigging and Seamanship*, London 1794

William Sutherland, *England's Glory, or Ship-Building Unvail'd*, London 1717

J T Tinniswood, 'Anchors and accessories, 1340-1640', *The Mariner's Mirror* 31 (1945)

Cecil Torr, *Ancient Ships*, London 1894

Thomas Traill, *Chain Cables and Chains*, London 1885

C van Yk, *De Nederlandsche Scheeps-bouw-konst Open Gestelt*, Amsterdam 1697

Guido Ucelli, *Le navi de Nemi*, Rome 1950

N E Upham, *Anchors*, Aylesbury 1983

Voyages en Egypt des annees 1579-1601, Editions Sauneron, Cairo 1974

Henri Waquet, *Histoire de la Bretagne*, Paris 1948

Nicolaes Witsen, *Aeloude en Hedendraegsche Sheeps-bouw en Bestier*, Amsterdam 1671

Index